Exquisitely Aligned

GINA MAIER VINCENT

Exquisitely Aligned

A POCKET GUIDE TO YOUR MAGNIFICENT FUTURE

WORLDCHANGERS MEDIA

Disclaimer: This is a work of nonfiction. The publisher and the author make no representations or warranties of any kind with respect to this book or its contents, and assume no responsibility for errors, inaccuracies, omissions, or any other inconsistencies herein. The content of this book is for informational purposes only and is not intended to diagnose, treat, cure, or prevent any condition or disease, including mental health conditions. You understand that this book is not intended as a substitute for consultation with a licensed therapist or practitioner. The use of this book implies your acceptance of this disclaimer. At the time of publication, the URLs displayed in this book refer to existing websites owned by the author and/or the author's affiliates. WorldChangers Media is not responsible for, nor should be deemed to endorse or recommend, these websites; nor is it responsible for any website content other than its own, or any content available on the internet not created by WorldChangers Media.

First hardcover edition: February 2025
Hardcover: 978-1-955811-83-5
E-book: 978-1-955811-84-2
LCCN: 2024917487

Edited by Bryna Haynes and Paul Baillie-Lane
Cover design and layout by Bryna Haynes
Cover artwork by Helen via AdobeStock
Author photo: Troy Jensen

Published by WorldChangers Media
PO Box 83, Foster, RI 02825
www.WorldChangers.Media

This book is dedicated to my children, Kai and Sonia,
my husband, Mark, and my parents, Karl and Linda.
Thank you for standing by me and always championing my "More."
It's an honor to be creating this life with you.

Table of Contents

Exquisitely
Aligned

*Take a stand for your beautiful, magical,
exquisitely aligned life.*

CHAPTER ONE
The Exquisitely Aligned Life

———◆———

I t was 2007, and life was good. *Really* good.

I was blissfully married to Mark, the man of my dreams, with two children: our four-year-old biological son, Kai, and our nine-month-old daughter, Sonia, whom we'd adopted from Guatemala just a few months prior. I'd left a grueling corporate career to stay home with our kids, and I taught yoga on the side because it was my passion. It seemed like we were on track for many more years of fabulous family life, and I woke up every day feeling grateful and content.

This is everything I want, I often thought to myself.

Then, suddenly, it all came crashing down.

In January, we discovered that Mark was suffering from polycystic kidney disease and that he needed to prepare for a transplant. His mother had died of a similar condition shortly after getting on dialysis; she'd been in her sixties but otherwise in good health. Mark had been having minor issues with his kidneys since before we were married, but we hadn't been expecting something this serious.

Mark got worse as the months passed. As a licensed family physician now specializing in life insurance medicine, Mark was able to stay on top of the discussions about his condition, but as he got sicker, it became my job to manage the logistics. I tracked and cataloged *everything* related to his appointments, treatments, and medications—and it was a good thing I did, because the hospital system in North Carolina, where we lived, seemed to be set up to fail us from the get-go. Our local transplant hospital told us they'd never received Mark's documents from the specialist, although the specialist's office swore they were properly submitted. This alone caused us months of delays.

And all the while, Mark kept getting worse.

In March of 2009, he had both kidneys removed in preparation for him to receive my right kidney six weeks later. During the surgery, the surgeon also decided to remove a very large cyst from his liver. They did this without asking or informing me. What's more, the surgery performed was high risk and came with multiple complications. The result was that Mark's liver failed, and I could no longer give him the kidney that could save his life.

The hospital denied anything had gone wrong. In fact, they outright denied that Mark was in liver failure. However, they kept postponing the kidney transplant.

I asked for a meeting with his entire team—the transplant surgeon, the liver specialist, the kidney specialist, and all the other people who were part of Mark's provider group. The answer I received? "We don't do that here." Each treatment was delivered in isolation and there was no overlap. The providers didn't work together, and even in this unforeseen and life-threatening situation, they refused to adapt.

It was an absolute freaking disaster. What kind of insane system didn't allow doctors to speak to each other about their patients? Were their regulations, procedures, and insurance standards really so important that they were willing to let my husband die in front of my eyes?

Mark urgently needed to be placed on the cadaver donor list for a kidney and a liver. His life was on the line. But no one seemed to want to take decisive action. It was all excuses and "wait and see."

My dreams for our future as a family began to crack. Then shatter. It felt like my entire reality was crashing down around me. I was unwilling to face the possibility of a life without Mark.

My dad used to say, "Gina, the squeaky wheel gets the grease." Up until this point, I'd been holding back a little, trusting the experts to do what was right for Mark, and praying as if our lives depended on it—because they did. But now? It was clear that business as usual was their priority. This hospital and these doctors didn't care about the exquisitely aligned life that Mark and I had dreamed of and designed. They didn't care if our kids would grow up fatherless.

So, I went full-on New Yorker. I documented *everything*—the pints of blood he needed, all twenty-seven paracentesis procedures and how much fluid was pulled from his stomach each time, and how he responded to the dialysis that he now required three to four times a week. I demanded answers. I said, over and over, both out loud and in my prayers, "See me. Hear me. Help us." I made advocacy my full-time job.

But, most of all, I took a stand for Mark's unlived future.

I took a stand for Mark seeing Kai become an Eagle Scout and graduate from college, even though he was only seven at the time.

I took a stand for Mark seeing Sonia dance competitively, graduate high school, and grow into a confident, brilliant young woman, even though she was only three at the time.

I took a stand for Mark and I walking hand in hand on the beach near our dream home in California, even though we were still living in North Carolina.

I took a stand for all the moments I dreamed would come to pass for our family—all the things that would never happen if I left Mark's life in the hospital's hands.

Mark needed me to take this stand. Our family needed me to take this stand. *I* needed me to take this stand.

Because, sometimes, taking a stand is what's needed to create and protect your magnificent future.

Once I decided to fully commit myself as an advocate for and defender of Mark, our family, and our dreams, I was instantly labeled as "problematic." When his care team wouldn't listen, or danced around the answers I was asking for, I raised my voice. I made myself heard. It got to the point where some of the doctors wouldn't even meet with me anymore. They would ask to speak to Mark alone and tell me I had to wait in the waiting room. Then, they'd pull me in and repeat what was said. I felt like there was a blatant campaign to shut down my advocacy, and I worried that my words and questions were being twisted.

We had to change the game. We had to get Mark out of this hospital system if we wanted him to survive.

So, instead of fighting to get the doctors in our current hospital to do the right thing, I started advocating for a transfer to the Mayo Clinic—which was nearly 400 miles away in Florida.

Finally, we were able to submit an application to the Mayo Clinic. We had to drive to Florida and stay for two weeks of testing. The response was encouraging: they accepted him for treatment, and seemed to think that, with time and a compatible transplant donor, they could help him recover enough to have a normal life. However, while waiting for donor organs, Mark would need to live within a four-hour drive of the clinic, which meant he couldn't stay in North Carolina.

On our tenth wedding anniversary, I left Mark behind in Jacksonville, Florida, at the home of a friend he'd known since his residency days, and set off back to North Carolina with the kids. As I watched their solemn little faces in the rear view mirror, I felt like my insides were freezing over. My husband was living on dialysis three states away from us, and my worst nightmare had become my daily reality.

Mark lived in Florida for thirty-nine days. His need for a new kidney and liver was so high that it bumped him up to the top of the transplant list. But even with that, he was fading. The mistakes made at the first hospital were causing even greater complications, and time was running out.

At home, I was trying my best to keep things normal for the kids, but it was hard. I was wracked with fear, frustration, and fatigue. Now that Mark was in better hands, all the energy I'd put toward advocacy had nowhere to go. My mind started running itself in circles; I couldn't tell whether I was coming or going. Sometimes, the fatigue was so extreme that I struggled to remember what day it was, or even what month.

On Sunday, November 15, 2009, I was sitting in prayer like I always did in the mornings—and my prayer was that someone would die today—or, if not today, at least this month. Someone young, with a healthy and functional liver and kidneys. Someone who could, with the gift of their organs, save Mark's life and let him come home to us in time for Christmas. Then, I realized that, in order for my prayer to be answered, there would be someone else, some other family, who would have to celebrate the holidays without their loved one—and I wanted to vomit. What kind of person had I become that I wanted to take away someone's son or daughter, niece or nephew, best friend, or even parent, so that I could have the life I'd envisioned with Mark? This was not who I knew myself to be. I believed in life. In love. In the exquisite perfection of divine design.

I was in a sick, sick place. I wasn't just fighting for Mark's life; now I was fighting for my own soul.

It was a wake-up call. A huge moment of choice. I could continue to try to force things to go my way, or I could "let go and let God."

A few days later, I took the kids out for Chinese food for dinner. I was so exhausted that I forgot my phone in the car. When we came out, I saw that I had missed multiple calls from Mark, and one breathless voicemail letting me know that he was being driven to the clinic by my brother—who, miraculously, happened to be in town doing some work for the friend Mark was living with.

"Mayo called. They have a match and want me to come to the hospital, but it doesn't mean it'll work. I met someone yesterday in the support group who was called eight times and is still waiting, so it may be a waste of time," he informed me.

On Sunday, I'd decided to stop praying for organs, let go of control, and let the Universe do its thing. Now, it was Wednesday, and Mark was getting a new liver and kidney.

I frantically began packing for a month-long stay in Florida. I called my parents, who, bless them, stepped up to take care of both me and our children while I focused on helping Mark recover. They arrived at my home at 9:00 p.m. While my mom settled in with the kids, my dad helped me pack the car. By 10:00 we were on the road, driving through the night to Jacksonville, where Dad would stay with me until Mark was stable. It was all adrenaline, but mixed in with the stress was a nearly heart-stopping flow of gratitude.

The workup started on Wednesday evening, and just after midnight, they took Mark into surgery. Eleven and a half hours later, he was recovering in the ICU. The surgeon was pushed to her limit trying to clean up the mess the doctors at the first hospital had made when removing the cyst from Mark's liver.

A good portion of the surgery was cleaning up the masses of scar tissue created by that first operation. She had to remove two and a half inches of his colon, and he needed a chest tube because part of the scar tissue had become attached to his lung.

"This is why we never remove those types of cysts on the liver," she told me later. "We know it causes liver failure, and it always creates complications later." While that was painful to hear, I was glad to have confirmation that my instincts had been correct: the first surgery had not only been unnecessary but had actually caused more problems than it solved.

The surgeon, and the whole team at the Mayo Clinic, treated Mark as a human being. They sat down as a team and discussed his recovery with us, and they worked together to make sure the choices being made were the right ones across the board. The body is an interconnected system, they said, and everything must work together in balance for healing to occur. I was never shut out, even when I asked hard questions. In fact, they routinely asked me what I was noticing and gave real consideration to my input.

About three months after Mark's transplant, we came in for a follow-up. I wasn't allowed in the treatment room because of the radiation equipment, so I sat in the second floor waiting room. I chose the sunniest seat I could find, and let the sunlight kiss the back of my neck. I pulled out my notepad and started writing.

I started listing all the things I'd given up over the last couple of years as I'd been caring for Mark and navigating the nerve-wracking path to his recovery. Cooking healthy food for the four of us, hosting fabulous dinner parties, going out to lunch with friends, walking, exercising, getting massages or a manicure. As I wrote, I realized that through no fault of Mark's or my own, I had set aside many of the things that made life feel good to me—that my idea of "normal" was no longer nurturing for me or my family.

Mark was recovering. Thanks to the organs of a forty-year-old woman, he would get to see our children grow up. We would get to take those walks on the beach in California. We would get to celebrate all the beautiful milestones and all the less exciting (but still just as beautiful) moments in between. If I wanted the rest of our lives to match up to the dream of our future I carried in my heart, it was time for me to step out of survival mode and take back the things that made life better—the little, joyful things that were the building blocks of an exquisitely aligned life.

A few days later, I bought myself a fun new apron, a new set of pots and pans, and some new cookbooks. I also bought some fresh flowers for the table, and I took my first step toward bringing the things we loved back into our daily lives.

From there, the joy just snowballed. Once I started doing things I loved again, I thought of more things I loved, and started doing those, too. Daily life went from being an obstacle course to being a celebration. Mark was home, he was healing, and we were going to be okay.

***

Before Mark's transplant, I thought I was designing an exquisitely aligned life for myself and our family. I identified the big things that mattered—being great parents to our kids, building lifelong memories, and taking great vacations—but I was a bit blurry on the details. However, all of that changed on the other side of this experience. If I wanted to design and live an exquisitely aligned life, I needed to stop thinking in terms of "someday" and start prioritizing "right now." Time was of the essence; as our family had so painfully learned, life could change in a heartbeat. I started looking more closely at how I was spending what I now refer to as my "Divine Resources"—my time, money, and energy. I now knew, viscerally, that these resources were not infinite—not for me, not for anyone—so I needed to use them wisely to create a truly exquisite life in the here and now.

Taking a stand for Mark in his healing changed me. I had never been afraid to go against the grain, but this was different. This felt like taking on not only a whole system of people and protocols that weren't working for us but also changing my perception of and relationship to fate and inevitability. I know too many people who, faced with the reality we were presented with, would have simply given up, believed what the first set of doctors were saying, and done their best to accept whatever came.

I surrendered to the Universe that Sunday in November, but I did so with a clear picture of what I desired to happen in mind. I may have surrendered the "how" of Mark's full and miraculous recovery to a higher power and let go of the "forcing" and wishing harm on others, but I never let go of my intention for the outcome.

This may seem like a small difference, but I believe it was the single most important piece of the whole puzzle.

Here's what I know. There's a life waiting for you—the one that's been calling you since you were small. The one that infiltrates your dreams and calls your attention exactly where it needs to be, especially when you least expect it. That life has called you here, to this book, to this page. You feel it, or you wouldn't have read past page one.

But here's the challenge: that life won't just "happen." It *can't* just happen, or it would have done so already. It needs to be stood for by someone who refuses to take "no" for an answer. It needs to be stood for by someone who believes in it so strongly that none of the "evidence" saying why it's impossible matters. It needs to be stood for by someone who refuses to believe the excuses. It needs to be stood for by someone who wants it badly enough that they are willing to do whatever it takes to create it.

That beautiful, magical, exquisitely aligned life needs to be stood for by *you*.

There are a million ways out of the destiny you were born for. There are a million "somedays," "maybe next times," and "if onlys." But there's only one way to have it.

You have to choose it. You have to choose it with every fiber of your being, with a conviction and certainty that makes it impossible for you to fail.

Your exquisite life hasn't given up on you, my friend. That's why you feel it, every day, calling you forward. It has chosen you. It has claimed you.

Will you claim it back?

Embracing Your "More"

This book was written with the intention to support you to define and design the future you desire and deserve. It's also my goal and desire to help you get rid of any barriers standing in the way of that process.

If I hadn't lived through Mark's health crisis alongside him, I might never have learned or appreciated the power of truly claiming what we desire. I've always been a go-getter, and I was already designing our ideal life before he got sick, but I was doing it in a more abstract, ephemeral way. I knew what I wanted and thought, "I'll definitely have that someday"— but, at the same time, part of me felt like I needed to accept that we probably wouldn't get everything I envisioned for us.

We had so much already; how could I justify asking for more?

It wasn't until our whole future was in jeopardy that I learned that there is a world of difference between dreaming about a great life and *making a deliberate choice to have it.*

A few years before Mark got sick, not long after our son's birth, I was chatting with a dear friend and decided to share something vulnerable from my heart.

"I just … want more for my life," I confided. "More than being a mother and a wife. More than what we have right now. I'm just not sure what it is."

I expected this friend, who had known me longer than my husband, to understand immediately. Surely, she too felt this vague longing! But her response was anything but empathetic.

"What are you talking about?" she blurted. "You have a beautiful home, a great husband, a healthy son, and you just got back from a crazy vacation in Italy. You have it all—and now you're saying you want *more*?"

Ouch. I fought back tears as the guilt came rushing in. Had she misunderstood? Did she think I wasn't grateful for my life?

What I know today, but couldn't articulate then, was that I wasn't looking for more boxes to check. I was looking for a different level of fulfillment. I just didn't understand what that could look like, or how to ask for it. If I'd known what my "More" was, I would have gone after it in a heartbeat. But I didn't—and since even the *idea* of me wanting more for myself was enough to bring out my friend's judgment, was it possible that I didn't *deserve* more?

After that day, I buried these desires deep down and kept them to myself. This quickly made me feel misunderstood, alone, and unworthy of my dreams for our life as a family.

It was this profound sense of unworthiness, more than anything else, that led me down a path of investigation and self-discovery. My research showed me that this unworthiness is nothing new; in fact, it's been passed down through generations by men and women alike, and by society itself. Somewhere between birth and maturity, we learn that it's not safe to communicate our desires.

But, here's the thing: unworthiness isn't healthy, helpful, or necessary. It leaves us trapped in a place where we cannot move forward. And that's no way to live.

In the journey of self-improvement, we often find ourselves caught in the paradox of gratitude and the unspoken desire for something more. In fact, the very thought of upleveling our lives and contributing to the world can trigger a massive wave of guilt, as well as a landslide of judgment from others. Perhaps we have more than enough to survive in the world, and fear being labeled as greedy or selfish. Or, maybe we struggle to define for ourselves what "More" truly means. Maybe we're saddled with spiritual questions about whether we "deserve" what we don't already have. But whether our guilt is self-generated or seeded by judgment from others is almost irrelevant. The real question is: can we be grateful for everything we've accomplished and created while still wondering, "Is this all there is?"

Yes. Yes, we can.

If you have a sense that something crucial is missing in your life, it's not because you're "bad," ungrateful, or selfish. It's not because you're "in your ego" or materialistic. And it's certainly not because you aren't deserving. No, you have a desire for more because your exquisitely aligned life is calling you, and *you are listening because you don't yet have what you want.*

When things got down to the wire with Mark's health and I decided to surrender the "how" of his recovery, I wasn't thinking about whether I "deserved" to have a fabulous husband and a joyful life for our family. I don't think he was having that debate with himself, either. He wanted to live. I wanted him to live. We wanted to create an amazing life together. And, each in our own way, we *claimed* that life, and refused to accept anything less than what we had chosen. When the doubt vanished, the miracles started showing up.

You are about to take a journey into your own dreams. Over the course of this book, you will define and design the future you desire and deserve. This journey will completely transform your relationship to yourself, your reality, and your power.

But, before we begin, I need you to do something for me. I need you to promise me, and promise yourself, that you won't give up—that no matter what happens, or what doubts creep in, you will keep reaching for the life that is calling you. That exquisite, beautiful, meaningful, fulfilling, joyful, magnificent life is meant for you, and you were meant for it.

Now, imagine that I'm taking your hand. I'm your guide through the darkness, doubt, and fear. When you can't see what's next, you can follow my lead, my words, my voice, and know that you are not alone.

Are you ready to get started?

Is "fine" actually enough to make life worth living?

CHAPTER TWO
The Myth of the "Ideal Life"

———◆———

In my twenties, well before I met Mark and we began building our family, I left my home state of New York for a job in Charlotte, North Carolina. This was exciting for me because Charlotte was sunny, warm, and far more affordable than New York City. Sure, it wasn't the fashion capital of the world, but I went from living in an illegal studio apartment in someone's basement on Long Island to having my own beautiful, one-bedroom apartment—on the same salary.

Needless to say, I felt like my life got an upgrade with this new position. However, once I got settled in, I found that this new role was not at all what I'd been expecting.

My new boss had also been relocated from New York to Charlotte, but while for me it had been an opportunity, for her it felt like a demotion. For some reason, the company felt like they couldn't fire her outright, so they created a "lateral move" to a place where they figured she could do less damage.

And boy, could that lady do some damage. She was miserable, and she made sure everyone around her was, too. She wasn't just rude; she was mentally abusive. It got to the point where I asked for a transfer to another department just to get away from her.

In the midst of this, my friend Marie met a guy when she was part of a friend's wedding in South Carolina, and she wanted me to meet him. "He's too young for me," she said, "but I think you'll like him."

And that's how I found myself on a date of sorts with Dave.

I knew, even then, that I wasn't truly ready for a relationship. When I'd left New York, I'd also left behind a boyfriend I truly loved. I had made the decision to prioritize my career, which my ex understood and respected, but my heart was still healing.

Dave was handsome, kind, and obviously into me. I knew right away that he wasn't my type, but I found myself attracted to the way he moved through life. He wasn't hyper-driven and career focused like I was. In fact, he was a bit of a couch potato.

After so much change in a short period of time, he felt … solid. Steady. Grounded. And I liked it.

This path also fit with my "checklist" for my life. Go to college? Check. Build my career? Check. Now, all I had to do was get married, buy a house, and start a family, and I'd be living the dream, right?

I was comfortable being with Dave. I loved him. I loved his family. We were both Catholic and had similar life goals and family values. We went to church together. We both wanted to be married, and the timing was aligned with our individual and mutual life plans.

Yes, being with Dave was good. But it wasn't *great*. It wasn't *exquisite*. I was settling, and part of me knew it.

Yet, when Dave asked me to marry him, I immediately said yes—mostly because I couldn't think of a good reason to say no.

Over the next several months of our engagement, I found myself … falling away. I didn't socialize as much. I stopped putting the same degree of effort into how I looked; although I was and always have been a fashionista, I found myself having less energy for it. I felt like I'd stepped into someone else's life.

Everything to do with the wedding was difficult. Nothing was coming together. Registering for gifts was complicated. I had trouble with the flutist I was trying to hire to play at the church. I couldn't settle on a cake design. I was frustrated with my smaller budget, because even though I had happily agreed to pay for the whole wedding, I didn't have enough cash to make it the day of my dreams. I felt like everything about this wedding was tighter and smaller and less amazing than I had dreamed of it being.

But the thing that really woke me up was when I stopped being able to look at myself in the mirror. I would avoid my own eyes while brushing my teeth. I wouldn't look at myself when I washed my face, or even while I was putting on make-up. I'm sure my lipstick looked … interesting most days. I didn't even want to see my own reflection in the car window when I put the key in the lock. I didn't want to look, because I knew I wouldn't like the person I was seeing. She was okay, but she wasn't *me*. She didn't dream my big dreams. She didn't have the adventurous, dynamic life I still desired.

There was nothing "wrong" with the woman I was becoming. She wasn't deficient or lacking or "less than" in any way.

But I would never fit comfortably in her skin; she would always feel too small to contain the true *me*.

Three months before my wedding, while I was working as a sales rep for Candie's Shoes, I worked a booth at a shoe show in Charlotte. When I got home, I asked Dave to come by (we weren't yet living together). He showed up with a bouquet of sunflowers and started cooking us a meal.

I looked at the box of our wedding invitations on the table, stamped and ready to send, and just blurted out, "On a scale of one to one hundred, how sure are you that you want to marry me?"

He took a moment to consider. "80 percent," he replied.

My whole body went cold. It was like I was standing in a morgue, and I was looking at my dream future lying dead and cold in the open steel drawer. It had been dying, I realized, for a while, but now I could see that there was no bringing the dream back to life.

"Dave, 80 percent isn't enough for either of us. We're only at 80 percent, and we're both young, happy, healthy, with no kids and no real stress. If 80 percent is all we have, this isn't going to work."

Right then and there, I called off the wedding. I told him to take the food and the flowers, return my key, and leave. And then, I sank to the floor and cried. I swear, I could feel my heart shattering in my chest.

The whole situation was devastating. Even though I'd been the one to call it off, I was still heartbroken. It took months to unravel all the plans we'd made, all the places our lives were entangled. I lost a lot of money on deposits and venue fees. Our families were hurt and a bit bewildered.

But I could look at myself in the mirror again—and that alone let me know that I'd made the right decision.

I realized, in the aftermath of this choice, that I had pigeon-holed myself into a life I didn't love without even realizing it. Marriage, home, and children were major life goals for me, and I wanted those things enough to try to make them work with the wrong person. Don't misunderstand me: I'm sure Dave and I would have had a nice life together. He was a great guy. He would never have hurt me or cheated on me. I know he would have been a great dad to any kids we had. It would have been fine.

But is "fine" actually enough to make life worth living?

I never considered myself someone who bowed to convention. I'd always been independent, fierce, and assertive. But somehow, the "norms" of society and my Catholic upbringing had gotten under my skin. I was the right age to get married. It was the right time. I was in the right place. On the surface, I was being handed every ingredient for an ideal life—and a big part of me felt guilty for not just … rolling with it.

The Pursuit of What's Expected

Back in high school, my friend's mom put together a scavenger hunt. I don't remember what the prize was, only that I was *so* excited about the prospect of winning. We had so much fun scrambling around town late into the night. By the time we returned to my friend's house with all the goodies we'd collected, we were laughing like maniacs.

We won, of course. I definitely did a happy dance.

But by the end of the night, I found myself wondering what the heck I was going to do with all the random stuff we'd collected. What were, at first, prized possessions quickly became miscellaneous junk that had little meaning. We'd found all the things we'd been instructed to find, but would they really add value to my life now that the game of acquiring them was over?

For far too many of us, life is like that scavenger hunt. We pursue and snatch up all the things we're told to collect: the college education, the respectable job, the "perfect" marriage, the big house, the nice car … you get the picture. But here's what no one tells us: simply achieving or acquiring these things doesn't automatically set us up to have an exquisite, extraordinary life. And, if we confuse the game of pursuit and collection with true fulfillment and satisfaction, we can end up with a jumble of stuff that looked fun and shiny from afar but in fact holds us back from what we truly desire and deserve.

Now, there's nothing wrong with wanting *all the things*—if those things are truly ingredients in your dream life. Despite what some people and philosophies will tell you, it's not evil or egotistical to desire more than you currently have in any or all areas of life. The problem is that, collectively, we are programmed to desire "ideal" things and experiences that may not be truly meaningful and useful to us on our authentic path—and then, when we discover that these things aren't truly *for* us, we are subjected to guilt, shame, and judgment.

From birth, we are bombarded with an abundance of external information. We're told what is "right" and what is "wrong," what "good people" do and don't do. We're told what to believe, how to act, how (and who) to love, and what we "should" want from life. Depending on what cultural and religious frameworks we were exposed to, our ideas of right/wrong and should/shouldn't may differ wildly, but the results are similar no matter where we come from. By the time we emerge into adulthood, most of us have been force-fed a blueprint for a "good," "worthy," and "admirable" life—and, all too often, that blueprint leaves little room for our own deepest dreams and desires.

Designing an exquisitely aligned life most often means letting go of—or at least radically upgrading—our internal blueprint. It requires us to become aware of all the places we are trying to follow the plan instead of following our hearts. Moreover, it requires us to become willing to face three big challenges that stand between us and our dream life:

- ♦ The Authority Paradigm
- ♦ The Conformity Trap
- ♦ The Identity Paradox

Once you understand how these three challenges have been stopping you from creating your exquisitely aligned life, you'll be able to recognize where you've been holding back and start taking meaningful steps toward creating the future you truly dream of and desire.

THE AUTHORITY PARADIGM

Who or what, exactly, dictates how you live your life?

There are two types of authority that govern our decision-making: internal authority and external authority. The authority we respect and submit to directly determines our ability to create our exquisitely aligned life. If we want to create a life and future that are perfect for us, we need to stop looking to authorities outside of ourselves for direction and validation.

An "authority" is any person, group of people, institution, community, or society that we recognize as having power over us and our decisions. In some cases, this is positive, and we willingly cede power in that area of our lives—for example, our collective agreement as a society to uphold the laws we have established. However, when we start referencing external authorities with regard to our key life choices (such as what career we pursue, what we wear, who we date, where we live, or how we engage in spiritual practice), we can easily lose the thread of what we actually want in the jumble of messages about what we "should" want.

Before you read any further in this book, I invite you to reject the notion that you were created, or are in any way required, to follow external directives. Instead, envision yourself as a unique soul having distinct life experiences to express your divine essence and uplift yourself and the world. Your true potential as a soul can only be tapped and expressed when you are operating in alignment with your inner authority—your inner all-knowing.

If you struggle to separate the messages of external authorities from your inner wisdom, you are not alone. Many people feel incapable of expressing themselves in a way that allows them to be heard, seen, understood, and appreciated. If this is true for you, it's likely that you've chosen one of two paths: the "pleaser" path, in which you go along to get along; or the "rebel" path, in which you make choices in direct opposition to the expectations of external authorities. Unfortunately, neither of these paths will ever lead to the true freedom, purpose, and alignment you desire. Only partnering with your inner authority and heartfelt desires can do that.

While conformity may garner attention, approval, and acknowledgment, there's nothing richer and more fulfilling than authentically showing up as the exquisitely aligned soul you are meant to be.

In this book, you'll learn how to begin to listen to this inner authority, and to differentiate it from your own fear and also from the voices of others that you've internalized. The journey begins with a resounding "Yes!" to living a life that resonates with your unique essence. This pivotal decision is the cornerstone of your transformative journey, requiring a commitment to self-discovery, authenticity, and a life aligned with your deepest truths. Saying yes to yourself is the first step toward a purposeful and fulfilling life.

The journey of internal authority is not just theoretical; it's a lived experience. It requires you to learn to tune out the noise, radically reorient your perspectives and paradigms, actively embrace your divine essence, and become the ultimate authority in your life. Only then will you be able to make the choices that align with your deepest values and express your authenticity in every facet of your life.

There are unique gifts and talents that only you possess. You were divinely chosen to express these gifts. Much of the time, external authorities require us to dismiss our gifts in order to keep the peace or make others comfortable. However, the longer our innate gifts remain dormant and unused, the harder it will be for us to find fulfillment, purpose, and real joy. We'll revisit the concepts of innate gifts and purpose in more detail later in this book, but for now, consider whether conceding to authorities outside yourself has helped or hindered you in your search for purpose, meaning, and freedom.

THE CONFORMITY TRAP

Many mistakenly believe that living the life they are destined to live involves trying harder, conforming, or meeting society's standards. They think that if they become "the kind of person" who has X, Y, or Z, they will somehow be happier or more fulfilled.

Self-improvement is great, and we absolutely do grow into better versions of ourselves when we commit to a personal growth path. However, when self-improvement becomes a scavenger hunt—a process of collecting bits of wisdom from external sources—it can feed right back into what I like to call the Conformity Trap.

The Conformity Trap is a prison formed entirely of others' judgments and expectations. It's directly related to the Authority Paradigm in that it positions the "shoulds" of your family, community, culture, religion, or society as superior to or more powerful than your own intuitive wisdom. When you fall into the Conformity Trap, it's usually because you've bought into the lie that only certain behaviors, achievements, or traits will produce the outcomes you want in your life—and the people around you have, consciously or unconsciously, reinforced that lie.

Here are just a few messages you might have heard as a child or young adult. If you bought into them, you may have felt the jaws of the Conformity Trap close around you.

- ♦ "In our family, we do/are _____, not _____."
- ♦ "Good girls/boys don't _____."
- ♦ "If you do _____, you will go to Hell."

- ♦ "You can't make money in that career."

- ♦ "If you don't do _____, you are a failure."

Your happy, abundant, exquisite life can only be created by becoming passionate about discovering and embodying your truest self. All the self-help books in the world (including this one) won't help you manifest your desires if you can't separate who you are from who others expect you to be.

While the advice "just be yourself" is everywhere these days, the reality is not quite that simple. Breaking out of the Conformity Trap requires immense courage, commitment, and self-awareness. You will need to work through and move past not only the judgments of others but also some of your own unhelpful beliefs.

Luckily, I'm about to show you how to do exactly that. By the time you're done reading this book, you will understand exactly what you need to do to step out of the Conformity Trap and start living in exquisite alignment with your own most magnificent future. But for now, let's take a brief look at why we humans judge, and how we can begin to change our relationship to the judgment of others.

Overcoming Judgment

Most of us have experienced the pain of being judged by authority figures, close friends, or even family. This can make sharing our personal desires intimidating, or even dangerous. It may mean that we hide parts of ourselves from others or go out of our way to avoid judgment by conforming to others' expectations.

The truth is, judgment comes from two places: fear and jealousy. Neither of which have anything at all to do with you, and everything to do with the person judging you.

People often fear and judge those who live outside of their personal "norm." They fear that doing things differently may upset some aspect of the established order or require them to shift a belief they currently hold. Additionally, they think that anything that makes them feel uncomfortable or uncertain must inherently be "bad." Think of the cultural uproar when, during the 1970s, women joined the workforce in huge numbers, challenging the established belief that women should not work outside the home. People feared a change in their way of life, and as a result, they judged women's choices vehemently.

Resistance to change, and the judgment it creates, is part of a bigger, more universal human fear: the fear of the unknown.

To some extent, I believe we all fear the unknown. When we can't see what's ahead of us, or when we don't have context for what's unfolding in our reality, it feels a little like bumbling around in a dark room. Will we step on something sharp? Is someone or something waiting to ambush us? What if we go the wrong way?

The difference between those of us who choose an exquisitely aligned life and those who remain in the Conformity Trap is our willingness to embrace the process of moving from the unknown to the known—from the old to the new—rather than resisting or judging it. Eventually, any new way of living will become familiar and comfortable, as long as we are willing to allow it to be *un*familiar and *un*comfortable for a period of time while the transition unfolds.

The second reason people judge each other is jealousy.

The courage required to live outside a one-size-fits-all paradigm is no small thing. So many people long to escape the rules and expectations of their society, community, or family group and live on their own terms, but aren't yet brave enough to do so. Just like my friend who went into full-on attack mode when I shared that I wanted more from my life, some people harshly judge those who are actively pursuing what they see as "impossible," "selfish," or just "too much."

When you make a choice to create a life on your own terms, you will start doing what others only dream of. You will start turning dreams into goals, generously sharing your gifts, and saying no to anything that doesn't line up with your greater vision. When this shift happens, some people in your life will cheer you on wholeheartedly. Others will try to shut you down rather than face their own feelings of inadequacy.

All of us have felt jealous of another at some point. On the surface, jealousy feels like wanting what someone else has, but if we look a bit deeper, we see that it also stems from a belief that we cannot or should not attain what we want for ourselves. Often, this stems from a deep-seated feeling that we are not "enough" to receive what we desire. But what jealousy *really* does is allow us to feel better about our current situation while bypassing any level of introspection. Why? Because introspection might require us to face an even bigger and more uncomfortable truth: that we want, and need, to change.

Once we understand that all judgment comes from a place

of "not enough" or a fear of change, it feels a lot less personal. We can have compassion for the people doing the judging, and free ourselves from any obligation to conform to their expectations. We can't control their fears or feelings, but we can free ourselves from any need to cater to them.

So, I invite you to leave behind the heavy suitcase of judgment you've been dragging around. Judgment has this sneaky way of creeping into our lives, making us second-guess our choices, stunting our growth, and robbing us of the joy that comes with upleveling. So, just make a choice to release it from your life like it's a helium balloon and watch your spirit soar.

Imagine a judgment-free zone where every decision and every step forward is met with a celebratory high-five from the Universe. Trust me, life feels a whole lot lighter when you're not weighed down by the opinions of others—or, worse, by your own self-criticism.

THE IDENTITY PARADOX

One result of living in the Conformity Trap is that our identity—our sense of "self"—is created by and wrapped up in external authorities and influences. For many of us, it can feel hard to discern the difference between who we truly are and who we have been conditioned to be.

Much of our identity comes, for better or worse, from our beliefs.

Beliefs are strongly held convictions about who we are, right and wrong, or the way the world works. Beliefs and belief systems are everywhere, whether they come from society, religion, school, work, family, or some other source. Some beliefs are passed down from generation to generation. For example, we have beliefs about age, gender, physical location, spiritual practices, what to do for a living, what to wear, what to eat, how to talk—even how to give birth, retire, and die!

But here's the thing: the fact that we believe something doesn't necessarily make it true. And, what's true for one person may not necessarily be true for another. However, what we believe, whether correct or incorrect for us, will always determine how we see ourselves, who we think we are, and what we think we're capable of.

That, my friend, is the Identity Paradox.

When beliefs we learned from external authorities or developed through experiences of fear and judgment are directly opposed to what our inner authority is directing us to be and do, we will often feel highly uncomfortable. We may not trust the inner voice that is directing us toward the "More" we secretly desire. We may have thoughts like, "I'm not the kind of person who can be/do/have that!"

Unraveling a false identity given to you by external authorities and others' fears is a process. It requires you to be willing to strip away all the rules, beliefs, and identities that don't actually belong to you, to get to who you truly are at a soul level. This takes a high degree of courage. I'm not talking about superhero-style, cape-wearing courage (although if that's your thing, go for it!). I'm talking about the courage to let your mind drift into uncharted waters, beyond the constraints of a world that begs you to conform.

From the "Ideal" Life to Your Exquisite Life

Imagine a place where your potential knows no bounds, and where limits are set only by the expansiveness of your dreams. This is where the magic happens.

This is *your* life.

Life is too short for accidental living. If you've read this far, you are ready to make an eternal shift in the way you express yourself, take in experiences, and dance through life—away from the external sources of authority that dictate who, how, when, where, and with whom you should be. The pervasive culture of conformity, external validation, and deferring to others has held sway for too long.

On the other side of the challenges we've explored in this chapter is a deeper, richer, more meaningful life. A one-of-a-kind life. A life you don't need to "settle" for. A life that lives, breathes, and changes along with you. You will become magnetic, attracting only those things that will benefit your destiny. The right people, experiences, resources … the list is endless. What's more, if you make this choice you will become a beacon of authenticity for others. You will embody the power of *true* free will, and as such you will inspire others on their journeys.

The journey through the challenges of the Authority Paradigm, the Conformity Trap, and the Identity Paradox is a necessary part of your growth. The discomfort you will feel as you observe and confront the ways these challenges have shown up in your life is exactly what is needed to spur you to growth. In the moments of discomfort, you will confront your limiting beliefs, expand your boundaries, and step into new possibilities. Embracing this discomfort does not mean resigning yourself to perpetual struggle, but rather recognizing that growth always resides outside your current comfort zone.

Creating an exquisitely aligned life is a dynamic journey, not a static goal. It's about continuously peeling back layers, exploring new facets of yourself, and aligning with your ever-unfolding truths. In this energetic shift toward transformation, you will learn to acknowledge, appreciate, and listen to your inner essence, responding to its messages and teachings. When you powerfully identify and honor your soul-level truths, your magnificent future will become inevitable.

Do you deeply see, hear, and value yourself?

CHAPTER THREE

Your "Superyacht" Life

———— ◆ ————

One day, while walking together in California's Dana Point Harbor, Mark and I came across a truly awe-inspiring sight: a superyacht named "Water Lilly."

Immediately, I saw a masterpiece. A floating work of art. This wasn't just a boat. It wasn't even just a yacht. It was a statement, a testament to the aesthetic ideal of what a floating palace could be.

As my mind drifted through the layers of its creation, I realized that Water Lilly wasn't just a vessel; it was also a livelihood for countless individuals. Designers, architects, interior decorators, craftsmen, and, of course, the captain and crew, all needed to combine their talents to create this floating symphony of elegance. It was, quite literally, the end product of a complex chain reaction of creativity.

By my side, Mark grumped. "Who the heck needs a boat that big," he asked.

Our opposing opinions ignited a conversation about perspective. While my husband saw impracticality, waste, and excess, I saw a testament to human art and innovation.

Both of us were correct. Obviously no one "needs" a boat that big. Just like no one "needs" a nice house, or a car they love, or a bucket-list vacation, or a big white wedding. But we aren't here merely to survive and get our basic needs met. We are here to thrive; to be in awe of life and living. For many of us, beauty, elegance, and luxury are substantial contributors to living in that energy.

In a way, the superyacht is a metaphor for your biggest dreams and desires. As we discussed in Chapter One, what you most desire in your life can often feel unnecessary or just "too much." However, leaning into not only desiring but also actively inviting your own superyacht (whatever that is) challenges you to release judgment (other people's or your own) about what you "deserve" and can have, and instead to sit in awe of the beauty of the creation itself. The invitation is to be courageous, to let your mind drift into a space where you can not only have that immense, amazing dream, but also let it be something that benefits your family, community, and the world.

Will you give yourself permission to think even bigger?

The "More" Your Heart Desires

When I awake and walk down the stairs from my bedroom, I see the colors, patterns, and furnishings of my home, and I feel like I've arrived. I value beauty in all things, and I have created a beautiful home for myself and my family.

When I sip tea in my yard, enjoying the view, I watch the hawks soar overhead and the dragonflies and hummingbirds buzz around my chair, and I feel like I'm deeply, meaningfully connected to the Earth and all its vibrant life.

When I'm on my paddleboard, balanced on top of the water, I feel free.

When I'm watching my children try new things, follow their passions, and connect with each other, I feel fulfilled.

When I'm in front of a microphone serving an audience, whether as the host of my own podcast, a guest on a podcast, or on a massive event stage, I'm grateful for the opportunity to be seen, heard, and valued for what I bring to the table.

When I support a private client to have a massive break-through in their life, I know I'm living on purpose and bringing my full self to the table.

When I consciously align my life, it feels like everything is in flow—like life is happening for me, not to me or around me. I'm guided to the right people, the right places. I know what boundaries I need to set, and where I can be flexible. I know what I desire, and what I no longer want in my life.

Yes, stuff happens in my life that I didn't anticipate or plan for. But because I know what my life is really about, even my "failures" are steps toward my destiny.

This kind of richness, fulfillment, and joy doesn't happen by accident. A life like this is designed at a soul level, deep within you, and brought forth not by doing more or pushing harder, but by stripping away anything that is not exquisitely aligned with that design.

There are unique desires written on your heart. When activated, they cause your heart to beat faster. They feel rich, fulfilling, and meaningful.

They are the desires that make you feel *alive*.

I call these your "More."

When you fully embrace and partner with your "More," you stop chasing short-term indulgences, authority paradigms, or conformity fixes that promise joy but never deliver. Instead, you start leaning into your unique gifts, perspectives, and values. You start living on purpose rather than by accident.

When you partner with your "More," you claim the freedom to shape your future in a new, more deliberate way. I think of it as a marriage of sorts—a partnership based in love, respect, and mutual support. Your "More"—and all the dreams, heartfelt desires, luxuries, beautiful things, and precious moments it contains—is your destiny. If these things weren't for you, you wouldn't desire them! When you recognize that these dreams and desires are longing to be expressed through you, and that they are there for a purpose—that they are, in fact, *your purpose*—you will at last know the road to your personal "happily ever after."

I firmly believe that the greatest force for good on our planet today is the person who aligns exquisitely with their truths and values, and who lives authentically every day. The person who knows what they want and unashamedly, unrestrainedly pursues and invites it. The person who walks the path of their true desires—not the desires instilled in them by external authorities. The person who is in love with their life not because life is perfect, but because their life is beautifully, elegantly designed to be a match for who they are and what they're here to do and create.

You become that kind of person when you embrace your "More" and align your life to your "More."

As you already know, this book is your blueprint for an exquisitely aligned life. Another way to say that is "a life where your heartfelt desires are prioritized and realized." You already understand the need to break free of judgments, external authorities, expectations of conformity, and false identities. Now, we're going a layer deeper, into the "why" of it all, so you can begin your journey into your exquisitely aligned life.

Authentic Validation

The desire to be seen, heard, and valued is common to every human being on this planet. This acknowledgment is a basic need—one that many of us, for various reasons, have not fully experienced in our lives. In our attempts to get our needs met, we likely developed many judgments, false beliefs, and conformist attitudes.

However, one of the first steps in accessing your dreams and heartfelt desires is to know—really, deeply know—that you are the only one who can meet those needs and tend to your precious heart.

Do you deeply see, hear, and value yourself?

Do you truly see yourself when you look in the mirror? Do you see the beauty of your face, your form, your eyes? Or do you diminish yourself, cut your wholeness into flawed parts, and think, "I'll never be enough?"

Do you pause and pay attention when your soul speaks? Do you honor your internal authority above all others? Do you make time for quiet stillness so you can really, deeply *listen*? Or do you listen to and act on what others say or teach, even when you know it's not right for you?

Do you know what's most important to you? Do you value your own innate gifts and talents as the unique contributions they are, and take steps to increase your skills where needed?

Or do you make yourself smaller in order to fit in, get along, or avoid intimidating others?

When you truly begin to see, hear, and value yourself, you will begin prioritizing and honoring your true self. This will open the door to your heartfelt desires. Authenticity is the source of all true beauty, integrity, and aliveness. When you finally allow yourself to be yourself—your true, amazing, beautiful self—you say yes to the whispers of destiny.

"Yeah, that all sounds good," I can hear you saying. "But how do I do that? How do I make the shift?"

Well, friend, you *choose* it. Right here, right now, you make the choice to listen first and foremost to your inner authority. To see yourself as beautiful, whole, and worthy. To value yourself and your Divine Resources of time, money, and attention. And, perhaps most importantly of all, to treat your life as a brilliant adventure worthy of your awe, your gratitude, and your excitement.

If life is your superyacht, who and what gets to join you on board? Where will this adventure take you?

Your "More" has been knocking at that inner door for a long, long time. It's time to let it out to play.

THE FIVE ELEMENTS OF
EXQUISITE ALIGNMENT

As we enter Part II of this book, I want you to remember that
the ultimate goal of our work together is to uncover, embrace,
and ultimately live by your dreams, heartfelt desires, and your
"More." Your inner wisdom will never lead you wrong.

There are many paths to the state of alignment in which
your inner knowing will speak more loudly than any other force
in your life. The path I'm about to show you is based on many
years of doing this work on an ongoing, practical basis for my-
self and my clients. If you implement these five elements, you
will be well on your way to a future that is exquisitely aligned
with your "More" and your authentic truths.

The Five Elements of Exquisite Alignment

1. Define your "More"

2. Say "yes!" to your truths

3. Honor your Divine Resources

4. Set the stage for your "More"

5. Follow the magic

If you put your focus on these five elements, your life will change rapidly and in ways you cannot currently imagine. They will reveal the path to your magnificent future and give you the courage and guidance to walk it.

The Unsexy Truth About Self-Reinvention

Before we dive into the Five Elements, I want to address the idea of self-reinvention.

Many clients, when beginning their work with me, express a desire to "reinvent" themselves. They don't like who they're being in their lives, so they figure they have to wipe the slate clean and start over. Most often, this comes on the heels of a major life event: a job loss, a change in relationship status, the death of a loved one, a move to a new city, or some other major upheaval. They're about to step into a new life, and they want to do so as a new version of themselves.

Now, there's nothing wrong with wanting a fresh start. But hearing someone say, "I'm reinventing myself," gives me a pit in my stomach.

First, "reinventing" sounds like something you do in a basement bunker while wearing a white lab coat and goggles. It doesn't sound sexy or enjoyable. In fact, it sounds like a *lot* of work. Is "working on yourself"—like you're a home improvement project or a broken toy—really on your wish list?

Even the definition of "invent" is a mismatch to creating exquisite alignment. To invent something is to create something that does not yet exist. But you already exist. Your soul, your truths, your dreams, your heartfelt desires … they all exist in the here and now. You don't have to go looking for them. You have already been created to a standard of exquisite perfection in accordance with a divine purpose. You are unique, different, and special. Why would you want to create a new *you*?

You are not broken, flawed, or wrong in any way. The systems and beliefs in which you've been operating may be flawed or simply less than ideal, but those have nothing to do with *you*—with the truth of you.

So, defining and designing your exquisitely aligned life is not a process of reinvention. Rather, it's a process of revelation—of stripping away what is *not* you, so you can reveal what *is* you.

Now, you can absolutely feel free to disagree with my approach. I'm not here to tell you what to think. But if you're feeling like you need to become someone else in order to have the life you truly want, I'd encourage you to run that one by your inner authority. Do you really need to change? Or do you just need to reveal? Do you really need to "be different," or do you just need to stop playing the roles others have expected you to conform to? Do you really need to "stop being" the current version of yourself to make others comfortable, or do you need to upgrade your inner circle and fill it with people who see your brilliance without the need for filters and conditions?

And, perhaps the most important question of all: will your path of reinvention move you closer to, or further away from, your heartfelt desires and the truth of who you are?

When you reconnect with your soul-level truths, recognize your gifts, honor your Divine Resources, and cultivate daily habits that support your exquisite alignment, you will remember that you are divinely created for a purpose. You are already perfect. *You are exquisite.*

From there, it's only natural to claim the amazing life that is your birthright.

And, if at some point you feel the need to reintroduce yourself to your friends and loved ones as the most aligned, authentic, beautiful, soul-led expression of *you* ... well, you can do so knowing that you haven't been reinvented. You've been revealed, revitalized, and re-aligned.

How does that feel, my love?

There is no "More" too big or too small, only what is aligned with your inner truths, and what is not.

CHAPTER FOUR
Define Your "More"

———◆———

My client Celeste used to say, "Someday, someday, someday."

She'd been a faithful wife to her husband for over twenty years. She was a doting mother of two, a phenomenal daughter and daughter-in-law to her parents and in-laws, and a beloved friend to many. She was also a successful dentist with a thriving practice.

But although Celeste had a good life, it wasn't a great life. Her daily activities and obligations didn't fulfill her the way she wanted them to. She knew that caring for her family and patients felt purposeful for her, but it was also leaving her exhausted. In fact, she was teetering on the edge of burnout, giving her Divine Resources of time, money, and energy to things that she wasn't passionate or even excited about, and having little left over for the things that *did* matter.

Celeste had a dream to travel the world. However, her husband had no desire to leave their California hometown. She'd convinced him to take some short beach vacations when their kids were younger, but the older he got, the more dedicated he was to staying put.

However, travel wasn't the only hot-button issue for Celeste and her husband. He simply didn't see life the way she did. He saw obstacles where she saw possibilities. He saw problems where she saw solutions. Anything she wanted to do that differed from his normal routine was shot down—including her desire to grow and expand her dental practice. He saw her desires as "too much" and as a hindrance to his own comfort and stability. For many years, she'd silenced herself to make him more comfortable—but the desire for her "More" just wouldn't go away.

Finally, just after their twentieth anniversary, Celeste began to realize that she wasn't being valued in her marriage, and made the brave and challenging decision to pursue a divorce.

When I met her, she was newly separated and floundering a bit in her newfound reality. On the one hand, she was finally free to pursue the "More" that had been gently nudging her for years. On the other hand, she now had even greater financial and time responsibilities as a single co-parent and was at a loss for where to begin designing her new life. She knew she wanted more wealth, more health, more time, and especially more travel, but wasn't sure where to begin. After all, "More" had been synonymous with "someday" for decades!

The real shift started with a conversation about her childhood. As it happened, Celeste had always wanted to take ice dancing lessons, but her parents' budget didn't stretch to those kinds of activities.

"Why can't you take ice dancing lessons now?" I asked her. "They must have adult programs."

"That's true," she mused. "Why not?"

And that was the snowball that started the avalanche.

Celeste signed up for ice dancing lessons, and also found other outlets for physical exercise. The more she moved, the more her health improved, and the more energy she had.

Next, we decluttered her office and home. Being a visual person, Celeste is easily distracted by clutter. Once we cleared out her space, she had more breathing room for her vision.

Then, she turned her attention to growing her dental practice. For a long time, she'd resisted hiring a second dentist, concerned at the cost and effort involved. However, when we sat down and did the math, Celeste realized that not only could she afford to hire a second dentist to support the practice, but that this new dentist's presence would free her up for the travel she'd been dreaming of for so long.

Today, Celeste is a happy wanderer. In less than one year, she's taken her college-aged daughter to the Caribbean and her son on a mission trip to Central America. She also spent the holidays in Europe with both of her children, fulfilling a bucket-list dream of shopping the Christmas markets in Prague and Munich and giving her kids a memory they'll always treasure. At the same time, she's increased her dental practice's net income by 11 percent, and has plans to grow it by another 18 percent in the next twenty-four months.

Celeste is intentional about her time and energy now. She's learned to say no to things that exhaust her, and has released a few long-term friendships that, on examination, were one-sided. She found and fixed financial and energetic leaks in her business. And, thanks to online marketplaces, her regular decluttering practice brings in some extra cash!

All this because she followed her "More." The journey hasn't always been easy, but for her, it's been worth it.

Define the Future You Desire and Deserve

You, like Celeste, have a "More" calling you. I know you do. In fact, I'd bet that you're more like her than you realize.

Celeste knew that she wanted more from her life. Once she took the time to define it, the action steps were clear and natural. Owning and putting energy into her desires was the first step to creating the magnificent future she desires and deserves.

You, too, have a purpose and a passion. But the path to expressing those things at the highest level isn't through drudgery and self-sacrifice. It's through the very "More" you've been pushing away and denying for so long.

When you define your "More," you honor the truth of who you are. When you pursue your "More" through aligned actions, you bring the greatest version of you to life.

The future you desire and deserve will only exist in the

realm of "someday" until you define it and align to it. And that is what we'll be doing together in this chapter.

Before we move forward, I want to offer a disclaimer: while Celeste's relationship with her husband was a block to defining and claiming her "More," that was a situation unique to her relationship. Unfortunately, it's a situation shared by many people, both men and women. However, not all relationships operate under that dynamic. Not everyone needs to step away from their partner to realize their "More." In fact, realizing your "More" alongside your partner can be one of the most beautiful things you will ever experience, because they will get to witness you in your full glory as a fulfilled, delighted, exquisitely aligned human being. For example, Mark and I might disagree on many things (superyachts among them), but we support each other unconditionally, and my "More" includes making our relationship deeper and more loving every single day. Seeing me happy makes him happy, and vice versa. So, please, don't proceed with the assumption that you will need to walk away from your intimate relationship—or any relationship—in order to do this work. Just know that when you invite in your "More," the right choices for you will always be revealed.

WHO ARE YOU TO WANT MORE?

As we learned in Chapter Two, a desire for more is often part-nered with a rush of guilt or shame. Who are you to want more when you already have what you need to survive (which, in itself, is far more than some others have)? Shouldn't you just be grateful and get on with life as it is?

If you're struggling with the fear of judgment or others' jealousy, go back and read Chapter Two again. Do your best to set aside the fear, if only for the next few minutes.

Then, ask yourself, "What will be the result if I *don't* act on this desire? What will my life look like in a year? Ten years? Twenty years? Am I willing to settle for that?"

Oof. I'll bet that one hit you right in the gut.

You want more because you are meant for more. It's right there, like a winning lottery ticket, waiting for you to step up and claim it. So, take a deep breath, and say it with me:

"I am meant for more. The 'More' I desire is the exquisitely aligned future that is waiting for me."

Well done. Let's move on.

WHAT IS YOUR "MORE," EXACTLY?

So many of our desires come straight out of the Conformity Trap. In many cases, we've been told what to desire for so long that, when left to our own devices, we have no idea what we actually want!

Moreover, most of us have had very few role models when it comes to living an exquisitely aligned life. It's not the norm to see someone unabashedly pursuing their heartfelt desires and prioritizing their own alignment above all else. But when you do see those people, you know them instantly. They're magnetic. Compelling. They glow from the inside out. They're the kind of people who make you say, "Wow. I want to walk through a room like that."

When you see someone living in exquisite alignment, it's natural to wonder what they're doing, and how you can do it too. However, you can't have what they're having in the same way they're having it, because you are beautifully unique! Instead, what you can do is ask and answer the questions that they asked (and answered) for themselves, so you can find the light of your own inner truth, and let it shine.

What Did You Give Up?

The first question I always ask my clients when they are ready to define their "More" is, "What did you give up?"

What did you love as a child that didn't follow you into adulthood? What did you give up to be the partner, parent, child, executive, leader, or friend you believed you needed (or were expected) to be? Take some time to journal about this. Did you give up your love of travel, like Celeste? Did you give up the fiery, decisive part of your identity in order to appease a parent or partner? Did you give up dancing, singing, or painting? Did you give up the time and energy you used to invest in self-care, exercise, or even good sleep?

Below is a partial list of things my clients have told me they've given up over the years. Let these spark your own memories and ideas.

- ◆ Horseback riding
- ◆ Dancing ballet
- ◆ Playing hockey
- ◆ Reading books I love

- ◆ Painting landscapes
- ◆ Travel photography
- ◆ Going out to dinner
- ◆ Journaling

- Financial independence
- Cooking gourmet meals
- Hosting elegant dinner parties
- Attending wine tastings
- Singing karaoke
- Taking road trips
- Sitting on the beach doing nothing
- Eating street food in the park
- Going to live music performances
- Knitting/crocheting
- Playing an instrument
- Writing poetry

As you can see, the things we give up in the course of our busy lives or at the direction of external authorities are often the things we find the most fulfilling. Doesn't that make you a little sad?

If it brings you joy, it belongs in your life. Period, end of story. So, make a list of everything you've let drop over the years, and ask yourself, "What can I choose today that will allow me to experience the fulfillment and joy I desire?"

What Are Your "More" Dreams?

In addition to the things you've given up over the years, there are probably things you haven't yet had or experienced that are showing up as desires for you. Maybe you want a gorgeous new home, or to start a family with your partner. Maybe you truly want to own a superyacht or go on a bucket-list trip to an exotic spot. Maybe your biggest desire is to get rid of all your stuff and go full nomad! When you think about being, doing, or having "it all," what exactly is the "all"? What aspects of that dream life excite you from the inside out?

That's how you know your "More" is for you!

Or, you approach it from another angle: what are you envious of? Envy is just desire that's been locked down by external authority. Once you set free the desire, the envy will vanish!

To help you really get clear on your biggest dreams, here are some questions to ask yourself. Answer them in your journal, in your phone's notes app, or just in your head—but no matter what, try not to hold back or make your desires wrong.

- ◆ When do you laugh the most?

- ◆ What do you daydream about?

♦ There is a natural flow in you, like water in a stream. How do you create your flow? How does it feel when you're not in flow?

♦ What is your definition of "blissed-out"? What creates this feeling for you?

♦ What is your definition of "wholehearted"? If you were living "wholeheartedly," what would that look like?

♦ What subjects, people, and places fascinate you, and why?

♦ If you could teach people anything, what would it be?

♦ What makes you feel most connected to nature and the environment?

♦ What new experiences would you like to have?

♦ How do you define beauty? What in your life is beautiful? Where would you like to experience more beauty in your life?

♦ What would you most like to accomplish before you leave this planet?

These questions are not intended to lead you directly to answers about your "More"—although they might. Rather, they are intended to point your mind in the direction of your "More," so that it can go to work excavating your true desires on your behalf.

Once you start journaling about or pondering these questions, you should fully expect to get sudden downloads or visions while driving, in the shower, or even in your dreams. This is totally normal. You've invited your soul to speak—and speak it will!

As you invite insights about your "More," I also encourage you to listen to the whispers of your body. When you consider an element of your "More," how does your body feel? At peace? Light? Lit up from within? Heavy, dense, or dark? Neutral? Tense? Relaxed? Let your body help you interpret the information your mind is receiving and providing.

The "More" Balance

So often, life gets lumped into two categories: work and life.

Work-life balance is a catchphrase that feels too general to contain exquisite alignment. I don't believe any of us should segment our lives, or think that we constantly have to weigh one part of our life against the other to achieve some sort of generic stasis.

That said, an exquisitely aligned life is balanced by default, because everything is in flow and unfolds exactly how it is meant to, when it's meant to. Rather than a pendulum that we're trying to bring into stillness, alignment is cyclical, with different areas of life requiring our attention, energy, and Divine Resources at different times.

I've noticed that many people tend to focus on three areas when they first start looking for their "More": work, finances, and travel. Those are all great places to start—but if you don't actually desire to expand your financial or work life, or take a life-changing trip, you may wonder if there's a "More" for you at all.

Expansion can happen in any part of life, including in the areas of:

- ♦ Love relationships
- ♦ Family
- ♦ Friendships

- ♦ Networks and communities

- ♦ Hobbies

- ♦ Learning and education

- ♦ Physical health and well-being

- ♦ Mental health

- ♦ Spiritual practice

- ♦ Nature, animals, and the planet

I'll bet you immediately found a "More" waiting for you in at least one category on that list. Whatever it is, write it down. Then, ask yourself how much attention and energy that area of your life is getting from you right now? How can you give that dream more love?

♦ *Exquisite Gem: Create Quiet Moments* ♦

As a yoga teacher for over a decade, I always knew when someone was new to the practice of yoga. The newbies never sit quietly on their mats. They're always fidgeting, moving around, doing perfunctory stretches, and basically trying to look busy. I say this with levity, but I really have a lot of compassion for people who can't sit still. I was the same way for a good chunk of my life. When your brain never shuts up, stillness is uncomfortable. Sometimes, even terrifying.

Many of us are so busy looking outside ourselves that we forget to take the time to be quiet and listen to what our inner authority is telling us. However, most of the answers you're seeking to life's biggest questions—like, "What am I here to do?" and "What is my true life purpose?"—can be found in the quiet moments. If you can stop moving for even a few breaths at a time, your truths will surface.

Quiet time can involve actual meditation or yoga practice, of course, but it can also be enhanced with tools like journaling, breathwork, chanting or singing, performing creative visualization, spending time in nature, etc. It's all about what works for you.

If you don't already have a "quiet time" practice, give yourself ten to twenty minutes a day where you have no distractions, no phone or tablet, and no tasks to accomplish. Put it in your calendar if needed. You can simply sit quietly and pay attention to your breathing, or you can use one of the tools mentioned above. You may be surprised at what knowing arises within you.

♦ *Exquisite Gem: Dare to Daydream* ♦

One of the best quiet time practices is actually daydreaming. Yes, the very sort of mental wandering you got in trouble for as a kid!

Daydreaming has been proven to help boost memory, increase empathy, and create greater clarity. It refreshes your mind so that you can solve problems and meet goals more easily. Most of all, it can help you visualize your "More" without all the mental distractions. After all, if you're just daydreaming, you can explore the outer limits of your heartfelt desires without having to do, say, or prove anything to others.

The great thing about daydreaming is that you can truly do it anywhere, without anyone the wiser! You can daydream at your desk, in the car, on the train, on a walk, or even while making dinner (just watch your fingers if you're using a knife!). If you want to up the visualization ante, create a "daydream haven" in a cozy corner with a comfortable chair and pillows. Add a candle or soothing incense, and perhaps some background music—whatever helps you get in the zone.

Although it's important to create space in your day for it, daydreaming isn't, and shouldn't be, a structured experience.

It's vital to let your subconscious mind roam freely. Observe what comes up for you without judgment, and keep a notebook or your phone handy to capture your insights. Tap into your childlike wonder, and let your mind show you the full range of its potential!

You Don't Need to Have All the Details

In the upcoming chapters, I'm going to show you how to work with your "More" and bring it into reality. The more you do this—the more you pull your dreams of "More" out of the space of "someday" and into the here and now—the more exquisitely aligned your life will become. It's amazing how quickly honoring your "More" can transform your entire experience of life and living!

At this point, you may have clearly defined your "More" as a big vision, a massive goal, or even a sweeping change that will affect every area of your life. Or, you may have a few smaller goals that you are super excited about pursuing. Both are wonderful! Sometimes, like for Celeste in the story at the start of this chapter, a small decision—like taking ice dancing lessons—can start a cascade of change that leads to a life you only daydreamed about previously. Sometimes, only a small shift or realignment is necessary to bring your current reality into exquisite alignment.

No matter what your "More" is, don't judge it. There is no "More" too big or too small, only those that are aligned with your inner truths, and those that aren't.

Also, don't worry about getting it perfect. After all, your idea of "perfect" originates from your current self and circumstances. When you place expectations and controls around your "More," you actually close the door on all of the exciting possibilities that you aren't yet aware of. Instead, lean into the experience and be open to whatever new and exciting opportunities for exploration, play, and joy come your way.

In the next chapter, we'll explore what your "More" reveals about your purpose, and how you can lean into the Universe's gifts to create that "More" with ease, grace, and joy.

What is possible when you say "yes"?

CHAPTER FIVE
Say "Yes!" to Your Truths

———◆———

One of my clients, Julie, came to me when she was in a very dark place. She was depressed, disconnected, and wondering if her life would ever hold the purpose and meaning she craved.

She had been working as a marketing writer for a large company, and she was feeling completely disconnected from any sense of pride or value in her work. She felt like she was "selling snake oil." Sure, the pay was good, but the allure of all the shiny objects was wearing off, and her world was feeling empty. This sense of isolation was compounded by an unfulfilling romantic relationship.

Julie had toyed with the idea of starting her own marketing and communications business. She signed up for coaching programs and spent tens of thousands of dollars on mentor-ships that only created more confusion for her. Because she didn't feel connected to her purpose, she couldn't settle on a direction for this (theoretical) new line of work. In the end, all the conflicting business advice only took her further away from her personal truths. She felt unable to trust herself or her intuition after being pushed in so many directions, and was struggling to find clarity about her next steps.

Before we met, she'd dabbled in a number of personali-ty profiling systems, including the Gene Keys, but she wasn't sure which pieces of information to pay attention to. When we started working together, one of our first steps was to help her utilize the information gained from these systems.

What we discovered was that Julie is, and always has been, a very social person. Being in her early twenties, she grew up with social media, and was used to communicating with indi-viduals and groups online. This was a big part of what made her great in her current marketing role. However, although online communication came naturally to her, she noticed that it was feeling very shallow and unfulfilling.

As we dug deeper, I learned that her grandfather was a

writer, and also that she loved reading romance novels. Since she was very young, she'd carried a secret dream of writing her own romance novel. She loved telling stories; in fact, stories were a big part of what brought her into marketing. However, she wanted to tell stories of her own making, not stories about a company whose product she didn't really care about. Social media was not the medium she really desired to use to express herself; books were much more aligned with her joy.

As we deepened our work together, Julie started to notice other patterns, too. She had a habit of putting herself in situations that kept her stuck. The wrong job, the wrong guy, the wrong friendships. When she ignored her intuition, there was a wave of unease, but she always talked herself out of the feeling, thinking, "But so-and-so says I should, so …" This also translated to the business coaching she'd received. She tried to formulate a business according to others' systems, and they were all misaligned. The business models she was exploring lacked the depth and richness she wanted to create through her gift, which is her ability to write compelling stories.

Today, Julie is working on her first romance novel and also launching a business as a wedding content creator. She will produce videos of depth and meaning for brides and grooms. This combines her passion for people, love, and social media visibility, and provides a product that people will treasure and share for years to come. She's also got an exit plan to get her away from her corporate job and move her into her business full-time. She has found her purpose, which is to inspire people through her writing and content creation. And although it will be several more months before she strikes out on her own, there's a light in the distance that's calling her forward.

"I was so close, and yet so far away from my purpose," she told me recently. "Aligning with my purpose was, like, a two-degree shift, but it changed everything!"

Another client, a nurse named Clarissa, had been working in health care for decades. In addition, she and her partner, Joe, had two teenage kids, two dogs, and a pet rabbit at home. Her gift of empathy and caring for others had become a burden. Some days, it even felt like a curse. She was exhausted, overworked, and totally overscheduled. Her commitments were pulling her in a hundred different directions at once, and she had no idea how to make it stop.

When we began working together, the first thing we did was

look at her gifts. She felt that she was absolutely on purpose as a nurse and caregiver but acknowledged that she was spreading herself much too thin. What she needed wasn't a change of focus, but a change in the way she was expressing her gifts.

After learning more about her life goals and heartfelt desires, I suggested, "Clarissa, what if you were to stop working nursing shifts and instead start a business to support other nurses who are suffering in the same ways you are?"

This was a huge breakthrough for her. She hadn't understood that her skills as an empathic caregiver could translate into a role as a leader, coach, and teacher. Within a month, we had designed a business model that would help her transition out of nursing within six to nine months and give her the time she needed to take care of herself as well as everyone around her. Her partner, Joe, was 100 percent on board. In fact, he offered to pick up the financial slack so she could leave her nursing role even sooner.

These days, Clarissa is a role model and mentor for nurses in her home city as well as across the country. She supports other caregivers to manage their various priorities in healthy ways. Her business is thriving, and she's even started consulting for hospitals and clinics whose nursing staff are experiencing high rates of burnout. Her unique gifts have always been front and center in her life, but she didn't step into her own exquisite alignment until she started using them in a way that also included caring for herself.

Uncover Your Purpose

Once you've identified your "More" and embraced your dreams and desires for your exquisitely aligned future, it's time to look at how you want to work, live, and express yourself inside of that future.

In other words, it's time to find the *path* for your purpose.

People like to make purpose more complicated than it actually is. However, purpose is actually quite simple: your purpose in this life is to express your unique gifts in a way that makes you feel happy, fulfilled, and exquisitely aligned. Purpose is you doing the things that fill you up from the inside.

Purpose can also look like:

- ♦ Life feeling effortless, like you're floating.
- ♦ Feeling like you make a difference every day.

♦ Being excited to get up in the morning and do the things you get to do during your day.

♦ Being paid generously for work that doesn't feel like "work."

♦ Creating a legacy you're proud of.

♦ Serving in a specific way or for a specific group of people.

♦ People wanting to support what you're doing or creating.

♦ Maintaining (or regaining) vibrant health and sustainable energy.

♦ Becoming magnetic to the people and resources who are meant to support you.

More than anything, living in alignment with your purpose is about saying "yes!" to your truths and saying "no" to anything that is not your truth.

I said purpose is simple, and it is. However, simple and easy are not the same.

In practice, finding and aligning to your purpose can involve some trial and error. The more you work on connecting to your inner authority and breaking out of the Conformity Trap, the easier this process will become.

There are many ways to connect to your purpose. However, I've found these three elements to be among the most potent:

- ◆ Identify your unique gifts

- ◆ Shift your mindset

- ◆ Follow aligned invitations

These three ingredients, when used together, mix beautifully to bring more purpose into your life.

Let's look at each of these in depth.

IDENTIFY YOUR UNIQUE GIFTS

You are as unique as your fingerprint, but this uniqueness goes way beyond your DNA. It also extends to your natural talents and skills—what I call your gifts. These innate talents effortlessly flow through you, yet they are often overlooked and underestimated.

Imagine these gifts as exquisitely wrapped presents on your birthday, eagerly awaiting revelation. Unveiling each layer exposes more surprises, helping you recognize that these gifts aren't solely for your benefit but should be generously shared with the world.

Most people I meet have only a vague idea of their gifts. They know that they're naturally good at some things, but they're unsure whether those things are special or unique enough to be considered "gifts." But I would encourage you to consider that what's easy and natural for you might be profound and transformational for someone else who doesn't have the same gifts you do! The reality is that your compilation of talents is both exquisite and exclusive to you. Sharing these talents draws others to you, inspiring them to explore their own unique potential.

Your unique contributions are what the world is missing, and by recognizing and sharing your gifts, you fill that void.

There are many tools out there that can help you zero in on your unique gifts. Some of my favorites are the CliftonStrengths assessment (formerly StrengthsFinder), DISC, Human Design, and Gene Keys. I've had clients who successfully used Western and/or Vedic astrology, numerology, the Enneagram, and numerous other personality typing systems. While I don't believe that any human can (or should) fully operate according to these blueprints, no matter how detailed, each of the tools I've mentioned can provide specific insights as to your natural gifts by sparking your awareness in areas to which you may not have given much attention until now.

Whenever I enroll a new client, I always ask them to take (or to share their previous results from) a CliftonStrengths assessment. When we address the topic of purpose, we look at what would change if they concentrated on using only their top five or ten strengths, rather than using energy trying to "improve" in areas where they don't naturally shine. There's often a lot of external authority and judgments buried in our desire to "be better" in areas that just don't come naturally to us!

As you engage with the tools mentioned above or others of your choosing, look for patterns. You'll likely see similar themes across all of your assessments. Follow those breadcrumbs and you'll find clues as to your purpose and the ways of living that will feel most fulfilling to you.

You can also journal on the following questions:

- ♦ What are you most passionate about, and why?
- ♦ Where has following your passion taken you in the past?
- ♦ What do you believe to be your life's purpose?

- What do you like most about yourself?

- What do others perceive your most valuable gifts and talents to be?

- What was the most courageous thing you've ever done? What did it teach you about yourself?

- Where would you like to be five years from now? How is it different from where you are now?

- If you did nothing but what you absolutely love to do, what possibilities would you see in your future?

The transformative journey begins when you acknowledge your gifts and put them into practice. The more you embrace your authentic self and share your talents, the more you will understand and align with your greater purpose.

SHIFT YOUR MINDSET

It's easy for your mind to start running in circles and catastrophizing when you decide to claim your "More." This creates a lot of mental stress and clutter, and puts up roadblocks in the form of negative beliefs that make it harder for you to see opportunities. Fearful speculation doesn't serve your "More."

Nor do blame, anger, shame, or resentment. It's perfectly natural to be visited by some or all of those things as you begin to reclaim your life from external authorities and prioritize your "More," but you don't have to let them move in permanently and take over.

Here's the thing: when your mind is full of negativity, it's like a cluttered room. There's no space for new ideas, thoughts, or feelings to come in. In order to make space for new, more positive thoughts and perspectives, you need to shift the stuff that's not helpful.

There are many, many ways to do this. I'm sure you probably have multiple books on your shelf that address exactly this. However, it's often the simplest techniques that are the most effective—for example, the one-minute exercise below.

♦ *Exquisite Gem: One-Minute Mindset Flip* ♦

One exercise I give my clients is the One-Minute Mindset Flip. As the late Dr. Wayne Dyer used to say, "When you change the way you look at things, the things you look at change."

There's always a dash of vanilla in the best chocolate. The opposite of anything is always present and available.

This exercise is one way to change the way you're looking at a person, situation, or belief, and therefore change what you're seeing.

Whenever you feel your mind getting cluttered with negative thoughts, sit down with an old-fashioned egg timer (or use the timer on your phone). Set it for one minute. Ask yourself, "Is what I'm feeling/seeing/believing really true?" Then, for one minute straight, without stopping, speak aloud the exact opposite of what you believe about the person or situation. If you're angry with someone, shower them with gratitude, love, or forgiveness. If you're disappointed, talk about how great this situation is and how beautifully it's serving you. If you're disappointed, talk about how this perceived loss is a total gift.

Again, you'll want to speak continuously, without pausing to think about what you're saying or to argue with yourself.

When the timer goes off, take a slow, deep breath in and exhale for longer than your inhale. Notice how you feel. What's different? Do you feel lighter? Less fearful? More able to continue?

Once you get the hang of it, this practice will totally shift your mental state and viewpoint around the "problem" you're facing and empower you to see solutions that weren't apparent to you before.

FOLLOW ALIGNED INVITATIONS

Once you open yourself to the exploration of your unique gifts and talents and make space in your mind for your inner wisdom to make itself heard, you will begin to receive what I call "enlightening invitations." These invitations will do one of two things: they will spark intrigue, interest, and intimidation simultaneously; or they will present you with an opportunity to say no to something that is no longer aligned for you.

Let's talk about the first kind of invitation: the intriguing, interesting, and intimidating kind. I call these the "3-I Invitations."

Once you become open to embracing your purpose and willing to let it guide you into your exquisitely aligned future, you will begin receiving opportunities that stretch you, challenge your status quo, and call you forward to become more than you thought was possible. Saying "yes!" to these 3-I Invitations is saying yes to God, the Universe, Source, the Divine, or whatever higher power your belief structure includes. This is your confirmation that you are ready to explore uncharted territory, embrace your gifts, and live authentically. When you say yes, you will set off a cascade of transformation that ripples into every aspect of your existence.

This is the sweet spot where we shift from being passive and reactive to being empowered.

When you say yes to a 3-I invitation, you're saying "yes" to exploring your gifts, sharing them with the world, getting out of your comfort zone, and taking a step closer to your exquisitely aligned life. You're telling the Universe that you are ready to accept who you are and the value you bring to the world.

The more you say yes to these invitations, the more exquisite they will become. Whether it's a new career opportunity, a chance to express your truest self, or an invitation to delve into unexplored territories of your spiritual journey, recognize the power in embracing these 3-I Invitations.

Acknowledge your fears, but do not let them dictate the course of your journey. Embrace the dance of intimidation and intrigue, for it is within this dance that you will find the transformative power to become your truest self. Every frightening invitation is a potential gateway to enlightenment.

However, not every invitation is a 3-I invitation. In fact, once you make the decision to embrace your unique gifts and listen to the guidance of your inner authority, you will likely receive invitations that are the exact opposite of 3-Is. These invitations will be tempting opportunities to keep doing what you've always done. I call them "status quo invites." Your job is to say no to these invitations, no matter how easy it might feel to give in.

For example, you might receive a referral for a top-tier client the moment you decide you no longer want to be in your current line of work. Do you take the client and stay put a little longer? Or do you say no, even though it's easy money?

Or you might meet someone who has many good qualities but also shows some of the same red flags as past partners who weren't aligned for you. Do you continue to date them, repeating your past patterns, because there's no one else on the horizon? Or do you take a stand for what you really want, even if it means staying single?

One of my clients has described this second kind of invitation as, "the Universe testing me to see if I really want what I say I want, or if I'm just full of it." Another phrased it as, "passing up 'just okay' for the possibility of 'amazing.'"

Both of the invitations I've just described provide beautiful opportunities to say a resounding "yes!" to your truths and step into a greater degree of alignment in your life. If you're not sure if an invitation is a 3-I invite or a status quo invite, use that quiet time to go within. Ask yourself, "What is possible if I say yes? What is possible if I say no?" And then, trust the answers you receive. Your soul always knows what to say yes to!

♦ *Exquisite Gem: "Yes" as a Practice* ♦

Every day, you make thousands of little decisions. Each of these decisions is an opportunity to say yes to your truth, your gifts, and your purpose, or to deny and move further away from them.

Saying yes to your truths is not something you do just once. It's something you do over and over again. At first, it can feel daunting, but with time, it gets easier. For me, saying no to people, opportunities, and things that are not exquisitely aligned with my purpose and my vision for my future is now as natural as breathing. Because I have put in the work to gain clarity around who I am, why I'm here, and what I'm creating, I know immediately whether the people, opportunities, and experiences that cross my path are for me, or not for me. And, if I don't know, I know to take my questions to my inner authority during my quiet moments and wait for the answers to come.

In the next chapter, I'll show you how to align your daily decision-making with what you've learned about your "More," your gifts, and your purpose, so you can stop wasting your Divine Resources of time, money, and energy on things that don't support the future you desire and deserve!

Every decision you make, large or small, is an act of creation.

CHAPTER SIX

Honor Your Divine Resources

———— ◆ ————

O ne of my clients, Debra, was going through a divorce after a long and tumultuous marriage.

When we started working together, she'd already found a new apartment for herself so her husband could stay in their marital home with their teenage children. She had a busy corporate job that consumed a lot of her time, so this made sense. But even though the custody arrangements left her with more free time than she'd had in years, she was feeling drained and unable to move forward.

"Where is all your energy going?" I asked her.

"I'm not sure," she replied. "I just feel … heavy."

We looked at all the places where she could be experiencing "energy leaks"—where people, things, and situations were demanding attention and life force that could be better used elsewhere.

Immediately, I saw three things. First, there were numerous relationships besides her marriage that had been impacted by her divorce. In particular, there were two friends who just didn't seem to know how to manage the situation. These were married women who were close with both Debra and her ex-husband, and who had kids her own children's ages. After the separation, these friends told Debra that they completely understood why she'd left … and then proceeded to grow increasingly more distant, exclude her from social gatherings, and criticize her to other acquaintances. Debra was reaching out to try to start a conversation, only to be met with vague excuses—or worse, silence. Debra was invested in continuing the friendships, but the constant effort to see and speak to these friends, try to explain herself, and clear the air was exhausting.

Second, Debra's new apartment, while beautiful and spacious, felt very cluttered and disorganized. Her desk, her countertops, her bedside tables, and even the window ledges were all covered in random stuff—paperwork, accessories, books, journals, unopened mail … you get the picture. It wasn't that the apartment was dirty or dusty, and the clutter wasn't overwhelming, but it was enough to make the space feel chaotic.

Finally, her finances were a bit of a mess. She'd finished untangling all of the major accounts, but there were so many little things still to take care of that she felt overwhelmed. She was paying numerous monthly bills and subscriptions for her ex-husband's home (i.e., Netflix, the cable bill, and insurance for the family devices) simply because she hadn't gotten organized with updating the accounts. She was also paying for services, media subscriptions, and memberships that she was no longer using or using irregularly.

Once I got the full picture, I sat her down and said, "Debra, you need to upgrade how you are spending your divine currencies of time, money, and energy. Once you do that, you will feel so much better. Are you open to doing this work?"

She immediately said yes.

The first thing we worked on were the tiny financial leaks. It took her a single evening to clean up her accounts and cancel the things she was no longer using. This saved her around $400 per month—money she could now put to use elsewhere.

The second thing we did was get Debra's home organized.

I supported her virtually to declutter her space and choose a new, brighter paint scheme for the main rooms. She organized her paperwork, bought organizers for the odds and ends that were taking up space on counters and tables, and cleaned out the nightstand on the opposite side of the bed from where she slept to allow energetic space for a new partner to come in. She also chose to get rid of furniture she'd taken from her old home that didn't work well in the new space.

Feeling much lighter, she was ready to deal with the friendships and reclaim the time and emotional energy she'd been spending there. We used my RISE Scale (which I'll share with you in detail later in this chapter) to get a picture of how these friends were truly showing up for her. It was clear that the energy being invested in the friendship was all on Debra's side. Seeing that helped her step away from the relationships without any blame, shame, or drama. Her "More" included beautiful, reciprocal friendships that nourished her and left her feeling uplifted. These women were not able to offer her that at this time, so she gently let them go.

"The amount of time and energy I got back once I was able to stop thinking and worrying about what they thought about me, what they were saying about me, if they still liked me and cared about me … it's been game-changing," Debra told me.

These days, Debra has cultivated a vibrant social group of people who share her interests. She has financial overflow and plenty of "fun money," and isn't shocked by her credit card bill every month. She loves her new home and is able to completely relax there now that she has "visual peace" instead of piles of clutter. She's not sure exactly where her "More" will take her, but, as she likes to say, "I'm off to a great start today—and I'll get to start again tomorrow!"

***

My friend, it's time to move from visioning to creating, from dreaming to doing.

This is where the rubber meets the road. You've defined what your "More" looks like (or, at least, your "More For Now"). You've connected to your gifts and your purpose. From this point forward, your only job when it comes to creating your exquisitely aligned life is to make sure every decision you make, big or small, aligns with and supports the magnificent future of fulfillment, joy, and abundance you envision for yourself.

This is a new strategy for decision-making, and it may feel challenging at first, especially if you're used to making decisions based on the rules defined by some external authority. However, I promise you that, if you apply what you're about to learn in this chapter to your life starting today—starting right now—you will start to see massive shifts in your reality in a very short period of time.

Your Most Valuable Currencies

Every decision you make, large or small, is an act of creation.

However, most of us don't think this way. We do and buy things not because those things are in direct support of our ideal future, but because of social pressures, a feeling of obligation, or just plain old habit.

It's time for that to change.

The most valuable currencies at your disposal are *your personal time, money, and energy.* The way you spend these currencies says a lot about what you value and what your priorities are—not only to other people, but to the Universe. I call these currencies your Divine Resources.

Used appropriately, your Divine Resources are powerful spiritual tools that can radically accelerate the process of creating your magnificent future. Misused, they are the key ingredients and perpetuators of a misaligned, unfulfilling life.

Let's look at each of these one by one.

TIME: YOUR FINITE CURRENCY

Most people give at least some thought to how they spend their money. But how do you spend your time?

Is your day filled with activities that light you up, bring you joy, and feel like needle-movers for you? Or are you spending your time doing work you dislike, spinning your wheels, or fulfilling obligations you don't actually care about?

If it's the latter—and I bet it is, at least to some degree—it's time to look at how you're spending your time.

Most of my clients are interested in living their purpose. They're interested in helping others and changing the world. This means that they often say yes to things like volunteer opportunities, extra projects at work, and doing little (or big) favors for friends. When they come to me, they're often exhausted, but they don't know how to stop doing the things that are filling up their schedules but aren't filling them up.

The first lesson in managing your divine resource of time is that *your time is yours*. You wouldn't tell your child to give away their toys on the playground every day if they were getting nothing in return. That would be silly. So why do you keep giving away your time to people, things, and projects that don't reciprocate? I'm not saying all of your time choices need to be transactional. You should absolutely donate your time to causes that matter to you, *as long as the fulfillment and joy you receive feels like an equal trade for what you're giving.*

Unlocking Time Wealth

When I was teaching yoga, I loved sharing an ethical teaching called the Yamas. These five principles or "controls" comprise the first stage of the eightfold path of Ashtanga Yoga. The third of those principles is *Asteya*, which means "non-stealing." Essentially, it's the same principle as the biblical injunction, "Thou shalt not steal." It means do not take what is not yours or what you do not need.

When we apply this to the concept of time, we can observe where we are "stealing" time from ourselves and others.

♦ When we are late, we steal valuable time from others.

♦ When we don't build in time between our commitments, we steal valuable time from ourselves.

♦ When we don't give ourselves free time and flexibility to take advantage of unexpected opportunities, we steal time from ourselves that could be used to create our magnificent future, deepen our relationships, or just experience something beautiful.

As we learned in Chapter Four, Celeste once believed that she couldn't travel because her time needed to be spent working in her dental practice. She was, in essence, "stealing" travel and connection time from herself and her children by not adapting in other areas of her life. Once she changed that, her time wealth would expand exponentially. When she looked at the numbers, she saw that applying a different divine resource, money, could alleviate this roadblock. Once she invested the money to hire another dentist to support her practice, she had time to do what really mattered to her. (And, by leaning into what was exquisitely aligned for her, she created more money, too!)

Your time is the one resource you can never recover. Once it's gone, it's gone; that's how linear time works. So, I invite you to get out your journal and answer the following questions about how you're spending this precious divine resource.

- ◆ Create a list of all the things you do in a day, a week, a month, a year. What takes up most of your time?

- ◆ What percentage of your time is spent doing things you absolutely love and find fulfilling?

- ◆ Which of your current time commitments feel obligatory, draining, or like a waste of your effort?

- ◆ If you had more hours in the day, how would you spend them?

- ◆ How many hours in your day/week/month are devoted to upleveling *you*?

- ◆ On a scale of 1 to 10, how aligned are your most common daily activities to your "More," your purpose, and your magnificent future?

- ◆ How much time do you spend on activities that are not aligned with, or even actively contradict, your "More"?

If your "More" is about freedom, it's time to stop saying yes to things that restrict your freedom. If your "More" is about greater financial success, it's time to stop doing things that don't make you money (or that waste the money you already have). If your "More" is about changing the world, it's time to stop doing things that don't support that change. If your "More" involves making time for creative projects like learning to knit, writing a book, or playing an instrument, it's time to stop spending your free time scrolling on social media or binge-watching Netflix and start using that time for creative endeavors. If your "More" is about a deeper relationship with your family, it's time to stop multitasking while you're with them.

♦ *Exquisite Gem: Flirt with Time Freedom* ♦

It's time to dance with the possibility of breathing room in your days, weeks, months, and years.

The best way to flirt with time freedom is in small, easy-to-manage increments.

As an experiment, try building in fifteen-minute windows before and after all of your appointments. Do this for only a week or so, and notice how your days change. Are you less stressed? Are you on time more often? Do you have more time to say yes to spontaneous invitations?

If you really don't enjoy having extra time in your schedule, you can always go back to your old ways. However, I think you'll find that a little time freedom goes a long way toward making space for your "More."

MONEY: YOUR POWER CURRENCY

Your money is your power.

So, what, and who, are you giving it to?

When you spend your money on something, regardless of what it is, you are investing in the existence of that thing. This is true for everything from daily necessities to your biggest purchases (like your home, your car, or a superyacht). You vote with your dollars. You support ideologies with your dollars. You facilitate empowerment or harm to people all around the world with your dollars.

Every time you spend money on something, you are saying to the Universe, "I want more of this to exist. I want more of this in my life."

Many of us—myself included at times—spend our money

on things we think will bring joy, only to discover that they weren't worth the hype. For example, you might really love your daily coffee from that coffee shop, but is it worth spending $2,500 a year of your divine currency for the privilege? (Yes, that's what you're spending if you invest $7 a day into premium coffee drinks.) Or are you going through that drive-thru on autopilot because you've always done it, and everyone around you does it? Does that designer tee shirt give you enough of a return on investment that it's worth $400 more to you than a tee from a small organic brand? Or are you buying brand-name clothes because it's expected in your social circle?

Now, I'm not presenting these examples as "shoulds" or to make you wrong. If your magnificent future includes enjoying the heck out of a quad white mocha latte with whipped cream every single day, go for it! If wearing that cool designer tee sparks conversations with people who support your magnificent future in some way, or makes a statement about your personal brand that increases your income, that's awesome. Trust your inner authority! It's only when we put our money into things unconsciously that our choices become a detriment to our exquisitely aligned future.

Your money is a tool for legacy-building—not only in terms of cash and assets to pass down to your children or family members, but in terms of the world you create with your habits. For example, the clothing industry is among the biggest polluters on the planet. If you are committed to preserving the planet, are you buying your clothes and accessories on consignment to give them a second life, or buying from brands that utilize recycled materials, organic fibers, and safe dyes? Do you use reusable coffee cups for those Starbucks runs? Do you buy your veggies at the farmers market instead of wrapped in multiple layers of plastic at the big box stores? Are you buying eco-safe paints for your home's interior? All of these are small choices. Some of them (particularly buying on consignment) might even give your wallet a break. But all of them send your power—your money—flowing toward things you value and want to see more of.

Unlocking Money Wealth

No matter how much money you currently have access to, consider how you can be more intentional with your money.

How can you allocate money for experiences that create lasting memories? How can you leverage money to create more beauty, harmony, and peace in your life? Are you being called to give yourself permission to think bigger and open yourself up to elegance and luxury? Or are you being called to pull back and spend your power currency with greater care and deliberation?

From now on, whenever you open your wallet or click "buy now," I invite you to ask yourself the following questions:

- ♦ Is this purchase fully aligned with my "More" and my magnificent future?

- ♦ Does it support my values and what I want for myself, others, and the planet?

- ♦ Is this purchase about instant gratification or long-term bliss?

- ♦ Will this purchase/investment light me up inside or leave me feeling darker?

- ♦ Do I align with the core values and aspirations of the company/person I'm purchasing from?

♦ *Exquisite Gem: Money for Your "More"* ♦

A simple practice to uplevel your alignment with money is to keep a $100 bill (or several) in your wallet at all times.

This $100 is not spending money. It's a promise for your magnificent future. From now on, whenever you open your wallet, you will always have money in there. The simple fact of seeing money—especially for visual people—tells your brain, "I have money!" every time you open your wallet to pay for something.

So, every time you open your wallet, say to yourself, "I have money." See the $100, acknowledge it, and speak it in your mind (or aloud, if you can), using whichever of the words offered feels authentic to you:

"I get to [vote/choose/decide/connect] how to use this money starting right now."

Then, ask yourself, "Does this purchase [honor/celebrate/support] my deepest dreams and desires?"

When you do this, every time you open your wallet is a new opportunity to remind yourself of your "More." And every time you choose in alignment with your "More," you are one step closer to the future you dream of and desire. You are energetically opening yourself to what truly matters.

That's a pretty big return on $100, right?

♦ *Exquisite Gem: Pay with Gratitude* ♦

When I pay my bills, whether online or by check, I always write "Thank you!" in the memo section. Why? Because I'm grateful to be making those payments! I'm grateful to the person or company who provided the service because it enriched my life in some way. And I'm grateful to myself for creating an exquisitely aligned life where I can pay my bills without stress or fear.

Expressing gratitude when you make payments takes no time at all, but it can totally shift your energy around how money flows in and out of your bank account.

Another piece of paying with gratitude is to stop asking for discounts, especially from individuals who are providing a service for you. When you value others' Divine Resources of time and energy, you will give yourself permission to do the same. Also, if you don't value something enough to pay full price for it, it probably doesn't match up to your "More" and your desires for your magnificent future!

ENERGY: YOUR INVISIBLE CURRENCY

Your third and final divine resource is energy—specifically, the life force energy you invest in various aspects of your life.

Every intimate partnership, every friendship, every work relationship, every interaction, every task, every goal, every new venture ... all of those require energy. In fact, every area of your life that gets your time and attention also gets a portion of your energy. Some of these energy investments will pay you back in spades with joy, abundance, gratitude, laughter, and fulfillment. Others may not be so balanced.

Here are just some of the places you may be investing energy in your life.

♦ Your marriage or intimate partnership

♦ Friendships

♦ Work/career

♦ Professional relationships

♦ Extracurricular activities/hobbies

♦ Volunteer opportunities

♦ Your home environment

Are your energetic exchanges in these areas positive or negative? Are there friendships that are filling you up that you need to give more time and love to? Are there work relationships that feel like they're sucking you dry? Are those volunteer commitments making you feel grateful and fulfilled, or are they just exhausting you? Are you spending enough time doing things you love?

Then, of course, there are areas of your life that will always be energy drains. These include, but aren't limited to:

- Constant or persistent negative thoughts
- Anxious obsessions or constant worry
- Gossiping about others
- Dwelling on fears (without taking action to change things)
- Judging others
- Complaining

Every time you engage in the above, you spend valuable energy that could be put to a more productive use. It's helpful to identify when something is wrong, but focusing on it without doing anything to change it will sap your life force and leave you exhausted.

For example, during a recent session, my client Rea brought up two key friendships in her life that were no longer serving her. She had grown up with these friends, and their connection was based in history more than any commonalities in the present day. Whenever my client spent time with these people, she found herself feeling frustrated, drained, and taken advantage of. These relationships weren't reciprocal. She was merely a sounding board for their judgment and complaining, or a set of helping hands when they needed support. They rarely asked her how she was doing. As a result, Rea found herself constantly in "fixer" mode with them, giving unsolicited advice to help them move away from their negative mindsets.

"I love them and wish them well," Rea told me. "But if I met them today, I wouldn't pursue a friendship. We're nothing alike anymore."

Yet, she felt guilty about cutting these people out of her life.

I asked her, "How much time are you spending with these friends?"

"A few evenings a week."

"What if you could get all that time and energy back?"

"I'd go out and meet new people I connect with more. I'd look for people who can lift *me* up."

We designed a plan for Rea to extract herself from these relationships. It wasn't easy for her; she didn't want to just ghost these friends, but she knew they wouldn't understand her point of view, and she didn't want to waste more energy trying to make herself heard. So, she simply told the truth, without any emotional overtones: "I'm sorry, but I'm not free tonight. I'm doing [insert activity], which is really important to me."

Eventually, the old friends stopped calling so much. Rea still sees them every once in a while, but on her own terms, and only when she has energy to spare. Because she's anchored in her "More" with regard to her relationships, she's able to treasure these old friends for who they once were to her, without investing energy into trying to change them.

When you are living in exquisite alignment, your energy level may fluctuate, but you will *not* be constantly tired, burned out, anxious, drained, negative, hopeless, or shut off from your emotions. If you are feeling that way, your body and spirit are showing you that something needs to change.

In the Buddhist and Hindu philosophies, the water lily has a special meaning. The water lily floats on top of the water, peaceful and calm, rolling with the movement beneath it but relatively undisturbed. However, its roots are anchored in the mud far below the surface. As its petals close each night and open anew each day, it's a symbol of resurrection, like a spiritual rebirth. So it is with the divine currency of your personal energy. When you are anchored by a vision for your magnificent future and your "More," you will float effortlessly along the surface of life. Without that anchor, however, you may end up far from where you want to be planted.

Unlocking Energy Wealth

You are the guardian of your inner flame. It's vital that you protect it fiercely. If you are not feeling like the most energetically charged-up version of yourself, it may be time to reassess your commitments and take a courageous stand to remove any energy drains from your life.

Your energy, even more than your time and money, is where you align with your "More." How you use your energy shows God, Source, the Universe, your loved ones, your family, your friends, and most importantly, you, what truly matters to you. When your energy is pointed toward what is most important to you and to your magnificent future, you claim your "More" with every breath you take.

The most powerful way to direct your energy is through *intention*. When intention becomes a part of your daily life, you will navigate each moment with purpose and awareness. You will pull back your energy from things that aren't in sync with your desires, and begin to create a life that radiates meaning and purpose.

So, take a moment to slow down, connect with your "More" and your purpose, and set an intention for the remainder of your day. Decide how you will direct your thoughts, actions, speech, and emotions toward what truly matters to you. Anchor in the deepness of your desire for a magnificent future, and choose from there. Remember, you already have every-thing you need to create that future. You don't need to give your energy to anything that is not aligned for you.

Then, when you wake up tomorrow to the sun shining, the birds chirping, or your loved ones smiling, recognize the gifts of another beautiful day, and return to your intentions. Who will you be today? How will you spend the currency of your energy? What will you *not* feed with your time, money, and attention? What will you say yes to—and where do you need to say no?

You can also ask the following questions each time you are called to commit your energy to something or someone:

♦ Will this be a positive use of my energy?

♦ How will I feel while/after I do this?

♦ Am I saying yes to this out of joy or obligation?

♦ Will putting my energy into this conversation/task/ relationship bring me closer to my "More" and my magnificent future?

♦ *Exquisite Gem: The "RISE" Scale* ♦

How are your relationships supporting your "More"?

Not all of the people in your life are going to be supportive, or aligned with, your "More." That's why I recommend doing a regular "relationship inventory " of all the people you see and interact with regularly using the "RISE" scale. RISE stands for Reciprocity, Integrity, Support, and Empathy.

Using the RISE metrics, give each person in your life a score between 1 and 5 for each of the following questions, with 1 being "not at all" and 5 being "absolutely!"

- ◆ ***Reciprocity:*** Does this person put as much energy into the relationship as you do?

- ◆ ***Integrity:*** Do you trust this person?

- ◆ ***Sincerity:*** Do you feel genuine, heartfelt support from this person in at least one area of your life?

- ◆ ***Empathy:*** Do you feel seen, heard, understood, and valued by them?

The answers that come to you will tell you a lot about the relationship and how you will choose to spend your energy with this person in future.

The key to doing this successfully is to keep the drama to a minimum. No matter the nature of the relationship, there's no need for blame, anger, resistance, and guilt (on your part). This isn't about them, it's about you and the kinds of relationships that match your vision for your magnificent future.

It's All About Your "More"

Examining how you're using your Divine Resources can produce some of the most profound "a-ha" moments in your alignment journey. When you do the math, it's easy to see exactly what you need to do every day to move into alignment with your "More."

Your Divine Resources are gifts bestowed upon you each and every day. How you spend them and renew them expresses what you want and what you value. Over the long term, the way we spend them will determine whether we end up with the life we desire and deserve, or whether we stay in a state of wanting and lacking.

Our Divine Resources can easily become off-kilter in our fast-paced world. So, pay attention. Every time you open your wallet or click "buy now"; every time you hire someone or bring on a partner in your business; every time you interact with your partner, friends, kids, or pets—heck, every time you swipe left or right—make sure you're doing it in a way that honors your time, money, and energy, and the "More" you deeply desire.

If you're not sure which path will best serve your "More," I have one more Exquisite Gem for you.

♦ *Exquisite Gem: Gain Clarity*
with a Bird's Eye View ♦

When you're dealing with confusion in a situation or relationship and unsure which direction to take, try to see the situation from above, as though you were a bird flying over the landscape. (You can also envision riding in a helicopter or an airplane.)

Close your eyes and imagine that you—your consciousness—are rising up out of your body. As you detach yourself from your physical body, you leave your emotions and stress, and the stories you're creating around them, behind.

Once you're floating above the situation, you can see what's really going on. Instead of seeing only what's right in front of you, you can see the landscape in every direction. If you take one path, it will lead to this destination; if you take the other, it will lead you somewhere different. Maybe one path will lead you closer to your "More" while the other leads away from it. Or, perhaps one path will simply result in less stress and energy loss than the other.

For example, I spoke to a client recently who was having trouble balancing her free time and her social life. Her friends and colleagues were pushing her to come to a big party where there would be over 100 guests, many of whom could potentially be good contacts in my client's industry. However, my client rarely drinks, is highly introverted, and values her alone time.

"Gina, I'm really stressed about this party," she said. "I don't want to go, but I worry that I might miss out on an important connection if I stay home!"

We did the Bird's Eye View practice. "Do you see the path that leads to the party?" I asked. "Follow it. What happens?"

"Well, there will be 100 people there and many of them will be drunk. Being around drunk people makes me anxious, so I will probably also drink more than I want to because of the anxiety. I'll end up leaving early because too much booze gives me a headache, and I'll feel like crap the next day, so I won't be as effective at work."

"Okay, what about the other path?"

"If I stay home, I won't drink. I'll get good sleep and be able to get through my list the next day."

"Which is more aligned with your 'More'?"

"The second one."

In the end, my client did not go to the party. She had no regrets. Her "More" is about spaciousness, self-care, and enjoying her solo time. Once she recognized that the pressure to attend the party was all coming from external authorities, and saw where each decision would lead her, the choice was clear, easy, and aligned. Six short days later, at another business event (which she inexplicably felt excited to attend), she met a business owner who immediately took a liking to her, valued what she had to offer, booked her, and paid in full.

The Universe rewards your exquisite alignment in ways you cannot imagine.

***

Only you know whether you are shepherding your Divine Resources with integrity. No one else can tell you what will, and what will not, create your magnificent future. Just don't make a habit of justifying misaligned choices to yourself. You *know* how harmony feels. Chase it. Require it. Demand it. And watch your world change!

In the next chapter, we'll look at how to build supportive daily habits so you can more consciously and productively apply your Divine Resources and make the meaningful shifts that will create your most incredible future.

Beauty, elegance, and luxury are always available to us. We simply must choose them, define them, and be intentional about creating space for them.

CHAPTER SEVEN

Set the Stage for Your "More"

M y client Sara, a journalist, was burned out.

In her early fifties, she had been burning the candle at both ends for years, and had developed some habits that were not nurturing her. Although her husband cooked, she often ate at her desk so she wouldn't fall behind. She listened to the news in every moment of free time—while on walks with her dog, at the gym, in the car, and even while "relaxing" at home. She told herself this was necessary in her profession.

To recharge her batteries, Sara planned one week-long vacation a year for her and her husband, and one for herself alone. But by the time she actually relaxed and began to enjoy these trips, it was time to come home.

When we met, Sara was experiencing escalating issues both

in her business and with her health. She was getting sick far too often—like, every six to eight weeks—and would need to take time off to rest. This resulted in her chasing her tail with deadlines. She was always running behind and then explaining to her editors why she couldn't deliver what was promised.

Sara thought the solution was to work harder and catch up—which was why she hired me. She thought I'd be able to help her be more efficient and productive—which, of course, was also my goal—but before we could work on the management of her Divine Resources, we needed to get her into alignment with her "More" and her purpose. And for that, we needed to create more space in her mind, her schedule, and her life.

My first suggestion was that she turn off the news any time she wasn't actively researching a story. I could see that all that negative energy was really draining her, and that she was giving those narratives too much space in her mind, body, and spirit.

My second suggestion was that she start to build mini-vacations into her daily and weekly schedule. This would give her time to go for leisurely walks (without music or newsreels playing in her headphones). This second habit was a game-changer for her. When we'd connected, she had expressed that she didn't like the new city she was living in. However, when she started taking walks without her headphones on, she started to notice the beauty of the neighborhood. She even met some of her neighbors, who quickly became friends.

The third change I suggested was that she start eating dinner with her husband—again, without the news on. This would give them time to talk about their days and reconnect over the delicious food he'd prepared.

My final suggestion was that she make time at least once a week to do something that brought her joy. This was a bit harder for Sara, but then she remembered how much she used to love horseback riding and caring for horses. I asked her to start exploring horse farms in her general area and also to ask her neighbors for recommendations. Within a couple of weeks, she was offered a gig to pet-sit a horse while the farm's owner was overseas. She was overjoyed.

Within a few months, Sara was seeing massive changes. She wasn't getting sick as often. Her stress levels were down. She was actually *more* effective in her business because she was rested, and her editors were commenting on how much more creative her articles were becoming. She was taking regular breaks each day, sitting outside, and walking several miles a day around her neighborhood. She was noticing that simple things, like sitting on her veranda, made her feel happy. She was more confident when networking, since she was once again at the top of her game career-wise, and the extra weight she'd been carrying was slowly melting off. Her energy was magnetic.

The space that Sara created in her life opened the door to her "More." Just a few small changes paved the way for her to receive everything she'd wanted but believed she hadn't had time for. When she made herself and her well-being a priority, everything changed.

***

I learned to create space for my "More" early in life.

For as long as I remember, I've been a fashionista. I didn't like the dresses that my mother bought me; they were all frills, lace, and flowers, and I wanted to be edgy and elegant. I also loved playing with hair and makeup and spent *way* too much time with my curling iron in middle school. No matter where I was going, I wanted to look and feel beautiful—but the Long Island weather always undid my careful work in about ten minutes.

As I got older, I said yes to whatever looked like fun: parties, social events, hanging with my girlfriends at the mall, taking the train to Manhattan … a lot of my time was consumed by play. So much so that it started to backfire. Between the hours I spent getting ready, getting to and from social gatherings, and actually doing the activities, I often found myself without enough time to complete my homework and other school projects, and I started falling behind.

I may be a social butterfly, but I'm also a perfectionist. There was no way I was going to let my grades slip just for more mall time. So, I made it a point to learn to balance having fun with my other commitments. I also learned that the magic happens when you're not looking for it, so I also started to leave space in my day for the unexpected.

During a summer trip to Europe before my junior year, I made the decision to cut my pin-straight hair short and stop wasting time trying to wrestle it into cooperation. That, plus better priorities around social time, freed up multiple hours a week in my schedule.

I attended the Fashion Institute of Technology in New York City, and I continued to be mindful of my time commitments.

Our instructors told us to come "dressed as if we were going to work," which in the industry means, "Dress like you're going to Fashion Week," so my short hair and good time management skills both served me well. We were also encouraged to find part-time work in the industry, which I did. I also made a mindful commitment to keep my busyness under control and stay open to any and all invitations that felt fun or exciting to me. After all, this was New York City, and anything at all could happen with a little bit of luck and good timing.

One day, my boss at my part-time job asked, "Gina, would you like two tickets to see the London Symphony Orchestra at Lincoln Center tonight? I can't make it, but I don't want them to go to waste."

Of course, I jumped at the chance. "Yes, please!"

Immediately, I called my friend Michelle. She was also free, so we dressed to the nines and headed off to the symphony.

The performance was wonderful—an inspiration. We left feeling like we'd been granted a glimpse into a bygone era. My boss's seats were amazing—we were front and center, just behind the orchestra pit. And all of it was free.

As we were leaving Lincoln Center, Michelle said, "Hey, the

Opera House is still open. Want to go look?" Neither of us had ever been in the building, and it was still early, so off we went. It just so happened that the night's opera-goers were enjoying intermission.

From a little distance, I heard my name. "Gina! Gina Maier!"

The crowd parted, and there was Ann, a buyer for Neiman Marcus whom I knew from my part-time job. She and her date were tired and asked if we'd like their seats for the rest of the opera.

"Sure," I said. "That would be amazing!"

So, she handed over the tickets, and in Michelle and I went.

What Ann had failed to mention was that her seats were in the fourth row. And that the person performing was none other than Luciano Pavarotti.

There was no way either Michelle or I could have afforded those tickets on part-time college salaries. And yet, here we were, enjoying some of the most amazing artistry on the planet.

It was a magical evening, made possible not only by the generosity of the people I surrounded myself with but also because I was a good steward of my time and energy. I intentionally left space open for the invitations that aligned with my "More," and this time it paid off beyond my wildest dreams.

I knew that my magnificent future included experiences of great beauty and art. But if I'd been too busy working, playing catch-up on obligations, or just not paying attention, I would have missed out on this amazing experience that brought my "More" into my "now."

Making Space for Your "More"

The stories I just shared are only two examples of why making space in your life is one of the most powerful practices at your disposal when it comes to your "More."

Space and time are the two key ingredients to creating—and living—your magnificent future. When you clear the physical and energetic clutter from your life, you make room for new and better things to come in.

Emptiness is not empty; it's space with potential.

So, commit to proactively designing your space (both mental and physical) with your magnificent future in mind.

The space you create should reflect the beauty, luxury, and elegance you want to experience. This creates a container that is fully aligned with your "More."

SAVOR THE SLOWDOWN

When I meet a client who is crazily overscheduled, one of the first things I ask them is, "Why don't you want to hear the voice in your head?"

Often, we overschedule ourselves because we are avoiding something in our reality—like a job that's no longer fulfilling us, a relationship that's not nurturing us, or a sense of guilt that we're not doing what we're "supposed" to. The busier we are, the easier it is to avoid sitting with ourselves in silence, because it's in the silence that those feelings of discomfort and misalignment arise.

Some people lose years, or even decades, to this avoidance. They're not intentional. They don't listen to what's truly important. They don't make the space to feel into what is aligned in their lives, and what isn't. And so, the opportunities to be more aligned, more intuitive, more spiritual, and more connected just keep getting kicked down the road.

So, build space into your week. Get used to listening to the little voice inside you. The voice that whispers about your "More." The voice of your soul. This might be uncomfortable if you have one or more areas of your life that are not aligned with the future you dream of and desire, but if you make the space to listen and lean into it, you will gain valuable information about what is yours to be and do, and what is coming from external authorities. In fact, I can practically guarantee that it was an external authority that told you busyness was a good thing in the first place!

♦ *Exquisite Gem: Step Away from Media* ♦

As I recommended to Sara, avoiding the news unless it's absolutely necessary can be a huge relief mentally.

You are building your own magnificent future. When your attention is constantly pulled from crisis to crisis (or, on social media, comparison to comparison), you don't have the mental and emotional bandwidth to focus on you. Moreover, studies show that excessive news media consumption has a negative effect on both mental and physical health, heightening stress levels and activating our fight, flight, and freeze response.

My rule is, if I can't actually do something about it, right now, from where I stand, my knowing about it won't help anyone. Making my world beautiful and supporting people in my community has a much bigger ripple effect than my outrage at worldwide atrocities or crimes I couldn't prevent.

That said, avoiding the news doesn't mean being passive. As we discussed in Chapter Six, our Divine Resources are our most important assets. You can learn about worthy causes, donate, volunteer, and vote without being glued to your news apps. And, if you're spending less time doom-scrolling, you'll have more time and space to do all of the above.

Trust me, if there's something you need to know—like, if there's an impending earthquake or a tornado is heading toward your town—you'll find out. Other than that, spend your attention like the precious commodity it is, and focus on making the biggest difference you can from exactly where you are.

MAKE TIME FOR TRAVEL

I've included travel under "making space" because it's something I believe everyone should make time for. If you're caught in a burnout cycle of monotonous work or family routines, you may feel stifled, uncreative, and unable to envision anything other than your current life. That's the exact opposite of what's needed to create your magnificent future—and travel is one of the quickest ways to break the cycle.

Travel is the antidote to monotony, stuckness, and overwork. We all deserve more beauty, freedom, and flexibility in our lives. We all deserve a break from the ordinary and a chance to breathe new air.

Depending on your current resources, "travel" might look like anything from a camping trip at a site thirty minutes from home to a five-star world tour. In terms of creating our "More," it matters less where we travel and more that we prioritize doing so.

Besides getting to explore new places, traveling has a host of hidden physical, mental, and emotional benefits, including lower stress levels, reduced disease risk, a sharper mind, expanded perspective, connections with new and old friends, and time in nature (to name a few). Most of all, it offers an opportunity to connect to your deepest truths and desires. There's nothing like living out of a suitcase, navigating a city in an unfamiliar language, or being awed by natural wonder to show you what's really important in life.

Invite Beauty and Luxury into Your Life

It's said that beauty is in the eye of the beholder, and it's true. What's beautiful to you may not be what's beautiful to me, and that's amazing. Beauty, by my definition, is simply a combination of visual, tactile, and sensory elements that pleases you. It's something we innately appreciate and desire. In fact, beauty is something we *deserve*. It fuels us, and supports us to be the best version of ourselves.

There's nothing superficial about beauty. Think about how you feel when you visit a beautiful building, see a stunning cityscape, or spend time in nature. There's a sense of awe, peace, excitement, and even joy.

Perhaps beauty and luxury fall into your mental category of "nice but unnecessary," or "only for people with piles of money." However, I beg to differ. Beauty and luxury have everything to do with creating your "More," even if they're not areas where you've historically chosen to put your focus.

Beauty allows us to relax, rejuvenate, and be inspired. It creates a higher and lighter energy all around us, and that affects us deeply at all levels.

Everything in our world has a vibration. Our eyes can't pick up the rate at which each person, animal, plant, or object is vibrating, but that doesn't mean we can't sense it in other ways. We feel it. Just think about the difference between walking into a nursing home versus a preschool. A birthday party versus a funeral. A hoarder's house versus a minimalist's. Energy may not be visible, but it's palpable.

You, your home, your workspace, your car ... all of these also have their own "vibe." Often, when I start working with new clients, we discover that the vibe—the vibratory frequency—of their home or office does not match at all with the "More" they desire to create. Some of it might have to do with clutter, but more often it has to do with beauty and luxury. When we encounter beauty, we feel uplifted. When we see discord, we feel tense. Your "More" will never be served if you feel stressed, disappointed, uninspired, or sad when you look in the mirror or around your home.

If you have not previously valued beauty in your life, I invite you to start now. Beauty has less to do with cost and more to do with how specific items or spaces make you feel.

Everyone, including you, is worthy and deserves to be surrounded by beauty, elegance, and luxury. There is an exchange between the object of beauty and the observer. You see it between couples in love, with museum patrons observing art, with music lovers at a rock concert, and with nature enthusiasts pretty much anywhere there's a sunset. This exchange is like super-fuel. It's inspiring, energizing, and transformational.

This is your invitation to express your beauty through your outward appearance, posture, and demeanor, as well as through your home and workspaces. Every time you beautify something about your life, it supports you in achieving your "More" quickly and efficiently. (Remember, I'm a New Yorker, so I love efficiency!)

Beauty, elegance, and luxury are always available to us. We simply must choose them, define them, and be intentional with bringing or creating space to call or invite them into our appearance, our lives, our businesses, our daily practices, relationships, and even our spiritual journey.

EXPRESS YOUR INNER BEAUTY

When you express your truest self outwardly, you become exactly what the world is missing.

Elegant and aligned self-presentation is a huge needle-mover for my clients. When you embrace looking your best, it can powerfully shift how others perceive you, as well as how you see yourself in any given situation.

Your appearance is the outward expression of your inner self. When authenticity threads through your clothing, accessory, and style choices, you're not merely adorning yourself; you're contributing to the collective beauty all around you. The beauty we create becomes a gift to the world.

Looking your best does not need to entail a huge budget, a complete closet makeover, or even a significant daily time commitment (although you can include all of those things if they align with and amplify your "More"). Really, it's a matter of intention, and of the story you want to convey to those you meet and interact with.

Here are some areas to look at when considering how to look your best.

♦ ***Personal style:*** This isn't about conforming to societal or group styles or values, but rather about allowing your clothing and accessories to reflect who you are and the "More" you desire.

♦ ***Color:*** Do the colors you wear every day enhance or detract from your radiance?

♦ ***Jewelry:*** Your choices in jewelry are punctuation marks that communicate your style, values, and intentions.

♦ ***Shoes:*** Do your shoes support you to walk through life with intention? Do they make a statement? Do they actually allow you to move, dance, and play?

♦ ***Fragrance:*** Scent is an often-overlooked detail. Choose a signature scent that not only pleases your senses but also sets the tone for your day. Like a melody, your fragrance lingers, leaving a subtle trail of your presence.

- ♦ ***Hair:*** Your hair is a crown you wear every day. A good haircut, chosen with intention, can be a powerful expression of your commitment to self-care. It's not just about style; it's about valuing yourself enough to present your best self each day.

- ♦ ***Smile:*** A smile is a gesture that invites others into your radiant world. Wear your smile as an accessory and carry it with you wherever you go.

Again, these elements don't need to require a huge investment of money, time, or energy. But if something as simple as aligning your outfit choice, haircut, or jewelry can make a world of difference when it comes to your "More," why *wouldn't* you make it a daily habit?

♦ *Exquisite Gem: Stand Tall* ♦

From a holistic perspective, our posture decides how we approach the world. So, do you stride into a room feeling attractive, confident, and powerful? Or do you slouch, hide, or try to disappear?

So many of us spend our days looking down—at our

phones, at our computers, at our tablets, or just at our feet as we're walking. We see our screens, or the ground, far more often than we see what's around us. This has the effect of narrowing our perspective and preventing us from experiencing the majesty of the world around us.

Standing tall can powerfully change your personal energy and help you not only present yourself in a more authentic and aligned way, but also improve your physical and emotional health. A tall stance reduces joint stress, wear, and injuries, laying the foundation for emotional and mental strength.

Next time you're standing or sitting in front of a mirror, do a posture check as you stand sideways in the mirror. Is your back straight, with your head squarely over your shoulders and hips? Are you leaning to one side? If you're standing, is your weight evenly distributed between both feet, and between your heels and toes?

If not, press your feet into the ground (or your glutes into the chair). As you ground down you'll find yourself lengthening upward as well. Enjoy the space you've just created in your spine and within your lungs. Next, roll your shoulder blades up, back, and down your back. Feel your heart open and the top of your head lift toward the sky. Notice your expanded perspective as your eyes take in the whole space. Take a deep, full breath, and notice the immediate difference in your energy.

Your body is now able to function more efficiently. Your heart is open. Your gaze is naturally lifted and so is your perspective. You're ready to step forward into whatever is next with greater confidence and joy. Not to mention the fact your "tech neck" wrinkles will soften.

Standing tall *always* beats shrinking for approval.

CULTIVATE BEAUTY AT HOME

Curating beautiful, elegant spaces at home and work that reflect your truths, desires, and personal energy will accelerate your creation process and support you in all kinds of ways.

Your home is your refuge. Our surroundings either support our journey in life or make it more difficult. They either raise our energy level or deplete us.

So, if your current living and working spaces aren't beautiful, where should you begin?

Start by decluttering and organizing as I've shared above. Get rid of anything that is no longer serving you. Repair anything that's broken or not functioning optimally—like the leaky faucet, the squeaky closet door, or the chipped paint on the trim.

Then, begin your beautification journey with the room in which you spend the most time, and where you'll feel an immediate reward: your bedroom.

You probably spend more time in your bedroom than in any other room in your house. Do you wake up inspired by your surroundings? Or do you see a bland, unexciting space— or worse, a pile of to-dos in the form of laundry, clutter, or even unread books?

To begin creating a more beautiful bedroom, start with intention. What do you want to feel in this room? Romantic? Sexy? Dreamy? Tranquil? Then, ask yourself, "What colors, shapes, furniture, and décor will support my desire?" Don't forget the finishing touches—sensory details like textured blankets and pillows, scents, and even live plants can all change the energy of your bedroom.

Before you begin, let me offer a disclaimer. I'm not asking you to go out and buy a new home or car that's more beautiful or luxurious than your current one. Nor am I saying you need designer clothing (unless that's your "More," in which case, consignment stores are going to be your new best friends). There are many easy, simple, and inexpensive ways to create uplifting energy for yourself and those you invite into your space.

So, if you can't currently afford new furniture or décor, it's time to get creative. If you take steps to declutter your home, you should have at least a few things to sell. Set aside those funds for décor items that suit you better. Search consignment stores, online resellers, even Craigslist and Facebook Marketplace. You can often find gems for free or close to free if you are willing to take the time to search.

Declutter Your Home

I often recommend a practice called Vastu to my clients. Vastu is an ancient Indian architectural and organizing practice focused on creating beautiful and harmonious living spaces. Similar to feng shui, it supports energy flow inside a space to support your goals and intentions, as well as your health, wealth, and vitality.

One of the primary principles of Vastu is the removal of unnecessary items from your space. Chances are, your home is full of items that you no longer use and that do not support or align with your "More." For example, I had a client who had a storage unit full of designer clothes that were too big for her. She had worked hard to lose weight and get healthy after years of being overweight and unhappy with her body. However, she was afraid to get rid of her old clothing, just in case the weight came back. When I helped her realize that holding on to her past was keeping her from enjoying her healthier, more vital future, she was able to release the clothing that no longer worked for her. Between consigning, selling on Poshmark, and selling items privately to friends, this client was able to fund a large part of her new wardrobe. Now, the fear of going back to her old, less healthy self doesn't crop up every time she pays that storage bill; instead, she is free to be a healthy, energetic, happy woman with a magnificent future ahead of her.

Make a habit of releasing items that you no longer use or that don't align with your "More." A good rule is, if you haven't used it in more than six months, it's time to let it go. Of course, there are a few exceptions to this—such as holiday décor or black-tie attire—but for the most part, if you're not using it regularly, it is taking up unnecessary space and energy and preventing you from searching for and acquiring the items that will bring greater elegance, luxury, and beauty into your life.

It's All for Your "More"

In the end, none of what I've shared in this chapter is about looking good to others from the outside. It's about setting the stage for your "More." When you have space in your life, your schedule, and your home, you have more room for synchronicities and aligned invitations. When you take steps to present yourself and your environment in the most beautiful way possible, you make room for even more beauty. Think about it as paving the road so your "More" can reach you more easily, or plowing the field so new seeds can be planted.

And, most importantly, remember that none of this needs to align with the rules of, or validation from, any external authority. Beauty, elegance, and luxury will present themselves in your life in the ways that you define them. If your friends, family, or colleagues don't understand or agree with your definition of beauty and elegance, don't worry. You are following the breadcrumbs toward your "More," not theirs. So, just stand tall, have patience, and remember that every shift you make in your energy and environment is inviting your magnificent future that much closer.

Even when we can't see it, even when circumstances and events seem to make no sense or even seem to be uncomfortable and challenging, we are always being led toward our exquisite alignment.

CHAPTER EIGHT

Follow the Magic

———◆———

I started working with a publicist to build my press room on my website a couple of years back. She challenged me to start writing articles to build out another aspect of my online presence.

I'll be honest: I didn't like this. Being a visual person, I generally prefer speaking to writing, and writing was a bit of a stretch for me comfort zone-wise.

Yet, I felt a nudge in that invitation. So, I started writing articles based on the first two seasons of my podcast and the teachings I was communicating there.

I was pleasantly surprised by the results. I realized that I had a lot more to say than I'd believed. This gave me the confidence to approach a local magazine, *Greet Coto de Caza*.

I presented to them two years' worth of monthly articles to pick from. They were thrilled and asked me to become a regular contributor. They had a half-year earlier featured our family as new additions to the neighborhood, so it was fun to work with them again.

Then, my friend Cynthia told me about Kym, the owner of two other magazines that I might be a fit for. These columns would allow me a bigger word count and more space to share my ideas. I jumped on that invitation, too.

A woman in my area named Cheryl had been following my articles for a while and reached out to me via email. "Hey! I love your message, and I'd love to connect you to some more like-minded people in our area." We met at her home, and I gave her my "Opening to Possibilities" card deck as a thank-you gift.

She connected me to a local couple with a similar mission and worldview. I've since been a guest on the husband's podcast and had him on mine. Next, I'll be meeting his wife to discuss being on her event stage.

All from a few dozen short articles I didn't want to write.

But wait, there's more.

Cheryl's gift to me at that first meeting was a book on calligraphy by Dr. and Master Zhi Gang Sha, who uses his spiritual practice of calligraphy to heal people. I read the book and liked what he had to say—especially the story of how Master Sha helped a renowned entrepreneur, David Meltzer, regain his lost wealth after a financial catastrophe. So, I started using the calligraphy for myself.

In the meantime, I invited Kym, the publisher of the other two magazines I'd been writing for, to lunch. During lunch I expressed that I wanted to find a charity I could lend my time and energy to. She connected me to one where the director and I immediately connected over coffee.

I was delighted to sign up quickly for an event. Immediately upon entering the venue, I met Tracy, a PR and branding genius who is now representing my brand. Within the first month of our working together, Tracy said to me, "Gina, I want you to start following this gentleman if you don't already know him. His name is David Meltzer and he has a podcast as well as live show on Instagram which I'd like to get you on."

Well, *of course* I had heard of David Meltzer, because I'd just read the book by Master Sha in which he shared his story. And, just before the publication of this book, I was invited to share my own story and mission on David's live show.

When we are nudged to take action toward our "More," it will often be in a direction we don't expect. I could never have predicted that writing a few short blogs and articles could have landed me a connection with a world-class PR representative or gotten me on a top live show. It just doesn't seem linear or logical. Yet, here I am.

The lesson? My exquisite alignment is unfolding even when I can't see it and don't understand it.

A similar thing happened again when I said yes to attending an event in New York with a coach in my network. I had been clearly guided to say yes to attending as a vendor, and I was looking forward to the weekend, but when I walked in, the atmosphere was … strange. It felt like everyone was on edge, including the people running the event.

During one part of the event, I went into prayer. I wasn't comfortable in the energy. I had no idea what to make of this. Had I been off-kilter before coming? Was something else going on?

And then, suddenly, I heard someone singing a mantra I

knew. It was the woman whose table was next to mine—a publisher and editor named Bryna. She was singing over the music to help balance the energy in the room.

I thought very little of it after that. I did take her card, though. And once I was home and had cleansed my energy of what didn't belong to me, I realized that she might have been the reason I was there. I knew I liked her and felt I could trust her. I knew, by her chanting, that our values were aligned.

On the other hand, I was clear that it was not yet time to write my book. So, why had I been pushed to go to this specific event, at this specific time?

I tucked Bryna's business card away in my closet and let it lie … until a year later, when I was cleaning out said closet and came across the card, which I had tucked away with a few other important items. Coincidentally, or maybe synergistically, I was finally ready to consider writing something more than my monthly articles. And so, the timing was perfect.

If I hadn't gone to that event more than a year prior, you would probably not be reading this book.

Our magnificent future is always being created—by us, and by the Universe, God, or whatever we identify as our

Source. Even when we can't see it, even when circumstances and events seem to make no sense or even seem to be uncomfortable and challenging, we are always being led toward our exquisite alignment.

Our job, therefore, is not to judge, fear, or get upset about things that don't initially go our way. I'll admit, in both of the examples above, I was a bit put out at first by being asked to step so far out of my comfort zone. But when I got grounded and looked back at what transpired, I could see a golden thread of intention connecting every experience. In the end, it was all for my benefit.

And so, let's dive into the biggest and most powerful secret to creating your magnificent future and your exquisitely aligned life: embracing imperfection.

The Beauty of Imperfection

In the pursuit of personal growth, there exists a paradox—one that defies conventional expectations and challenges the very notion of "manifestation." The paradox is that the destination is always aligned, but the journey rarely meets our definition of "perfect."

To understand this, we need only look at Mother Nature, a great force and an even greater teacher.

When I was in college, I took an art class that completely changed my worldview. Our teacher revealed a truth that resonated deeply with me. Nothing in nature, not one single thing, is perfectly symmetrical. No face, no flower, no tree, no leaf, no creature, no mountain, no cloud in the sky is perfect—or even exactly the same from all angles. Nature is imperfectly perfect, imperfectly beautiful, and imperfectly exquisite.

Imperfection, my teacher explained, is not the absence of beauty. It is the *essence* of beauty.

Yes, the most perfect, intricate, interdependent design we can fathom in our existence is completely, totally, unapologetically imperfect.

External authorities encourage us to focus on our weaknesses and to see anything less than "perfection" as flawed. We touch up photos of ourselves before posting them on social media, and then worry that when we meet people in person, they'll think we aged overnight. We change our outfits three times before leaving the house, only to find that our clothes look and feel different when we're in motion than they do in our mirror selfies. We share only the "good" parts of life with those around us, thinking that to do otherwise will make us look weak, incompetent, or "needy." We are focused on our shortcomings, when, in fact, our imperfections are what make us who we are.

Why do we expect "perfect," anyway? Honestly, wouldn't "perfect" be … boring?

When we identify our "More," find our gifts and purpose, and start creating change in our lives by managing our Divine Resources and developing supportive daily habits, we may end up accidentally cultivating an expectation that our journey will be linear, predictable, and smooth. As if our actions and feelings are a set of ingredients that, when combined in the right order, will produce a consistent product for us to enjoy.

Sometimes, it works that way.

But most of the time, it doesn't.

When we make our magnificent future and alignment with our "More" our priority, we need to be willing for it to get a bit messy. Sometimes, we're going to end up in places that don't feel comfortable, be asked to do things we don't want to do, or have conversations we don't want to be having. We may not immediately be able to understand why we were so strongly called to these experiences. We may not ever understand. But we need to trust in the imperfection of the journey, because it is always, and I mean *always,* for our highest good.

One of the best side effects of embracing imperfection is greater authenticity. When you stop trying to make everything perfect, you will be more present, and start enjoying yourself. When you stop trying to *be* perfect in order to force a specific result, you will become more of who you are. Authenticity attracts experiences and people that are aligned with your soul energy, your true gifts, and your true purpose. It's also attractive and relatable, because it's so wonderfully, imperfectly human.

Just like your magnificent future and your "More" are one of a kind, so too will be your journey into that future. Don't expect your road to look like anyone else's. Be prepared for the unexpected. The less you sink into comparison or seek validation, the more you will learn to trust both yourself and your journey.

So, as you move forward into your own exquisite alignment, embrace imperfection in everything, including yourself.

Celebrate your uniqueness. Focus on your strengths.

Be authentically you.

And remember, imperfection is not the absence of beauty; it's the essence of it.

Facets of Radiant Resilience

Imagine yourself as a rare and exquisite diamond. A gem that sparkles with brilliant light, representing resilience and strength. You are, indeed, precious—a unique gem in the vast universe.

Indulge me for a moment with science 101. As you may know, diamonds, contrary to their radiant appearance, start out as simple coal. Dark, black, and opaque, coal is the result of layers and layers of natural debris accumulated and compressed over years. Think of this debris as your life experience.

Deep under the surface of the earth, an alchemical process begins. For coal to metamorphosize into a diamond, two crucial events must occur. First, the carbon in the coal must reach a scorching temperature of 2,200 degrees Fahrenheit. Second, it must face immense pressure—approximately 725,000 pounds per square inch!

This is not an easy transformation. It's a slow, intense process that mirrors the challenges life throws our way. The pressure we feel to conform, to fit into the schemes of external authorities, to please others, to be liked and accepted—it's all part of the journey. Those pressures can either fracture us and grind us down into dust, or they can transform us into something *more*.

You may feel, when you begin your journey of exquisite alignment, that you are in this dark place. You may feel the pressure bearing down on you. You may feel trapped by internal or external forces, or both. Know that, when you feel this way, you are not being punished. You are in a crucible of transformation. You are being refined, clarified, and sharpened into a gem that more brilliantly reflects the "More" you are here to experience.

This is not intended to change who you are. Just like the diamond, you are already perfect, and that perfection exists even within the coal. What is required is to exist within the crucible in such a way that it makes you stronger, more resilient, and more refined. What is unfolding now is preparing you for the "More" that is just around the corner. When you're ready, your brilliance will shine through for all the world to see.

Living with Full Permission

"Can you tell me, on a scale of one to ten, where you see yourself as far as being worthy?"

My client Janet's eyes immediately filled with tears. "Four," she said. "It's a four."

I nearly fell off my chair. This woman was an absolute powerhouse. A PhD-level psychotherapist, she owned multiple businesses, had a thriving family and a dynamic social life, and presented herself as cool and confident in pretty much every situation.

This obviously had nothing to do with her accomplishments, and everything to do with her perception.

"What do you need to feel worthy?" I asked her gently.

She was silent for a moment. Then, she said, softly, "Permission."

Oh, this happens so, so often. We have all the puzzle pieces in place. We're ready to lock in our magnificent future and rise like a meteor into our next level of exquisite alignment. We're poised on the brink of a life that feels amazing ... and yet, we never quite cross the threshold, because we are still waiting on someone, or something, to give us permission to shine.

If you're feeling this need for permission, I'm giving it to you now. I'm giving it to you a thousandfold. You have permission to be fully you, to invite your "More," to share your gifts, and to manage your Divine Resources according to what is exquisitely aligned for you and your beautiful soul.

You have permission.

See? Wasn't that easy?

If you're still feeling a bit of hesitation, I understand. And I have some practical tools for you.

First, try to see yourself through other people's eyes. People who love, trust, and support you. Pay attention to the compliments they give you. In fact, write them down at the end of each day so you can revisit them. What are people telling you about yourself? Do they see you as being worthy of having your dreams? I'll bet they do.

I asked my client Janet to consider this. "What does it feel like to consider what people are telling you about you?" I asked.

She made a face. "Awkward," she replied.

"Why?"

"I just don't feel like it's true."

"Okay. Do you see the people saying these things as being honest and trustworthy? Or are they habitual liars?"

She laughed. "They're not liars."

"Good. So, believe them. What they're saying is true."

Once Janet started tracking what people were saying about her, she started to notice some themes. People saw her as warm and inviting. Even her office felt "friendly"—which can be unusual in her industry. She quickly went from a four to a six on her personal "worthy" scale.

When she started to implement what we were working on in other areas of our coaching—in particular, her management of her Divine Resources and her daily habits—she noticed another bump in her "worthiness meter." After a month or two of consistently caring for herself and keeping healthy boundaries around her time, money, and energy, she woke up one day feeling like a ten.

That day, she called me to say, "I'm giving myself permission to go for my 'More.' It's time."

Take a Stand for Your Exquisitely Aligned Life

———————— ◆ ————————

All those years ago, I took a stand for the life Mark and I wanted for ourselves and our family. I refused to let events or my own fears get in the way of our "More." And while it hasn't always been easy or smooth, in the end, all of the beauty we envisioned for our day-to-day has come true.

It wasn't a wish that brought us here. It was a choice—a choice we made, and continue to make, again and again.

Right now, you are standing on the precipice of the same choice. You can choose your magnificent future, or you can choose your status quo. It's up to you.

You now have all the information and perspective you need to choose your "More" and go for it. And, in the end, the only permission we need to step into our magnificent future comes from within us. What you've learned in this book is a tried-and-true pathway to this kind of liberation. If you're a student of spiritual principles, like I am, much of what you've read in these pages may seem simple, even elementary. But I promise, if you follow the road signs I've laid out for you in this book, your life *will* change for the better, and in ways you can't even imagine yet.

It's time to take a bold, brave, uncompromising stance for your magnificent future—just as I declared my future with Mark all those years ago. Take a stand for what you dream of, what you long for, what you desire, and what you love. Take a stand for the beauty, luxury, joy, fulfillment, and adventure you can't even imagine yet, but that you know in your heart is coming. Your declaration, commitment, and actions will cause a ripple effect in your reality that is profound.

So, give up your "somedays," and choose your "More" today. Trust me, you won't regret it.

Also, keep in mind that there is no "right" way to go about creating your exquisitely aligned life. You don't have to get it perfect. If you're feeling paralyzed by stress or expectations, start slowly, in a playful and curious manner. Think of a child being in awe of something amazing, rather than a world-weary adult trying to prove something.

Finally, remember that your future starts today, but it also extends out from here into the rest of your life. There is no rush, no deadline, and no urgency except your own desire for more. That said, you can always go further and faster with support. Investing in your future through aligned coaching, mentorship, courses, retreats, and healing work can smooth the path and help you avoid the roadblocks.

Now, love, I'll send you on your way—off into the sunset and the magnificent, exquisite future you desire and deserve.

May you never deny yourself the blessings of your "More," and always give your heartfelt desires the chance to blossom.

May you always believe in your inner wisdom, and place your soul's truths above all other authorities.

And, most of all, may you create a life of exquisite beauty, elegance, abundance, joy, fulfillment, purpose, and love—in all the ways that are meaningful to you. When you live in this way, you live as a light in the world.

Many blessings, today and always,
Gina

Resources

For more Exquisite Gems, visit
ExquisitelyAligned.com/gems

To invite Gina to speak, email
Speaking@ExquisitelyAligned.com

Listen to the Exquisitely Aligned Podcast on
your favorite listening platform or at
ExquisitelyAligned.com/podcast

Find the Exquisitely Aligned video series on Experts
and Authors TV at **ExpertsAndAuthors.tv**

Stay in Touch

ExquisitelyAligned.com

ExquisitelyAligned

@exqusitelyaligned

GinaMaierVincent

@ExquisitelyGMV

exqusitelyaligned

Acknowledgments

Heartfelt thanks go out to …

Bryna Haynes, without whom this book would not have been possible. Your guidance made my dream of writing a book a reality.

My clients—past, present, and future—for trusting me with the sacred journey to uncover their soul-level truths.

Mary Lou Davidson and team for amplifying my voice around the world.

Lynette Hoy for stretching me to put pen to paper and write articles.

Kerrianne Cartmer-Edwards for bringing the Exquisitely Aligned brand to life with your creative vision.

Tracy Keyser and team for helping me shine on a global stage.

Jim Niswonger for helping me solidify the strategy and structure of my systems for Exquisitely Aligned.

My husband, Mark, son Kai, daughter Sonia, and all my other loved ones and friends: thank you for cheering me on.

I am grateful.

About the Author

Gina Maier Vincent is a visionary thought leader, master motivator, inspirational speaker, author, and empowerment entrepreneur. A true New Yorker in her drive, captivating energy, and vivacious love for people, she was born and raised on Long Island but now calls Southern California home. As the oldest of three siblings and the daughter of an immigrant parent, Vincent is a self-starter who illuminates what others cannot see, and inspires change. Her life has been a journey that prepared her to help others design the future they desire and deserve, and today she guides people all over the globe on how to live *exquisitely aligned*.

Graduating from the Fashion Institute of Technology in Manhattan, she majored in Fashion Buying and

Merchandising, then later earned a second degree in Marketing: Merchandise Management. Gina's professional path began as a Buyer and Product Development Manager in New York City with Belk Store Services. She then moved on to become a leading Sales Representative for Candie's Shoes before taking a sales position at TransUnion. In 2003, Vincent discovered her true passion for helping others when she started teaching yoga and working with people to make life-changing mindset shifts. Then, in 2017, she began living with intention by launching her company, Blissed-Out, Fit and Feisty, LLC, which offers holistic services for body, mind, and soul. Under this umbrella, she is the visionary Creatrix behind Exquisitely Aligned, a three-step proven system offering a personalized, soul-shifting concierge experience. This service guides high achievers in aligning their time, money, and energy with their true purpose. Her strategies empower clients to create the future they desire and deserve, ensuring they make the most of their valuable resources.

Vincent's entrepreneurial endeavors have attracted a global audience through her *Exquisitely Aligned* podcast and the *Exquisitely Aligned* show on Experts & Authors TV. Vincent has also become a dynamic speaker in high demand, captivating audiences with her compelling messages and profound insights. As a takeaway, she offers her "Opening to Possibilities" card deck with valuable journal prompts and mindful, thought-provoking questions designed for people to reconnect to their truths. In addition to her many media appearances, she pens a monthly empowerment column for *Newport Beach Living Magazine*, titled "From Impact to Inspiration."

In her spare time, Vincent actively engages with her community by volunteering for nonprofits, paddle boarding, exercising, and entertaining. She cherishes her family and is a devoted wife and mother who celebrates significant milestones such as the natural birth of her son and the international adoption of her daughter. Her passion and intentions are deeply personal, forged through the twists and turns of her life. Having discovered her uniqueness and value at a young age, and then becoming a health advocate during her husband's serious illness, she now offers help to others to make profound transformations.

Today, Vincent continues to inspire, motivate, and guide individuals toward their most magnificent future. Her mission is to help others exquisitely align their lives.

About the Publisher

Founded in 2021 by Bryna Haynes, WorldChangers Media is a boutique publishing company focused on "Ideas for Impact."

We know that great books can change lives, topple outdated paradigms, and build movements. Our commitment is to deliver superior-quality transformational nonfiction by, and for, the next generation of thought leaders, conscious entrepreneurs, creatives, healers, and industry disruptors.

Ready to write and publish your thought leadership book with us? Learn more at **WorldChangers.Media**.